virtue makes sense!

virtue makes sense!

Mark E. Petersen
and Emma Marr Petersen

Published by Deseret Book Company   Salt Lake City, Utah 1973

Library of Congress Catalog Card No. 73-81621
ISBN No. 0-87747-500-8

Copyright 1973
by
Deseret Book Company

Lithographed by

DESERET PRESS

in the United States of America

CONTENTS

Chapter One

"LET
YOURSELF
GO?"

☐ "Do you really think there is a God, Judy?"

As he asked that question, Danny Gordon looked hungrily into the dark blue eyes of Judith Anderson.

The young couple had been sitting in Danny's little sports car for more than an hour as Judy resisted his advances, and finally she explained why she wouldn't allow him to take liberties with her.

When they got down to serious conversation, Judy told her boyfriend of the teachings of her parents and of her church and told him that to yield to his advances would violate the deepest principles of her religion, which she loved very much.

"Religion? Why bother with religion?" Danny argued. "Religion is for the birds and maybe for some old people, but even lots of them are dropping it.

"Why, do you know," he went on, "so many people have quit our church that it had to merge with the one over on Olive Street, and they are different denominations, as though that mattered. People just don't believe in religion like they used to, and if there's nothing to religion, then why bother with what it says? Why not let yourself go and have fun without all those outmoded pious restrictions?"

Judy smiled as she said, "Danny, you're just not talking my language at all. Your religion may be on the way out, but mine is blossoming."

Then it was that Danny asked his frightening question, "Do you really think there is a God?"

Judy was shocked as she listened to him. When she thought about that question, it seemed to challenge all she held dear. Was there really a God? She had never so much as raised the question in her mind before. The existence of God was something she had always taken for granted. Without doubts or qualms she had simply accepted his existence as one of the undisputed facts of life.

But now Danny challenged it. Of course, if there is no God, there certainly is no point to religion. And if there is no point to religion, there surely is nothing to all of its laws and restrictions. Was Danny right? Should they just let themselves go?

Deep in thought now, she was in no mood for further argument with her boyfriend. She simply told him to take her home, which he did.

As he drove away from her house, alone in the car, Danny too was more thoughtful than usual. Judy was completely different from most of the girls he dated, and he liked her.

What if there is something to her religion? If it made Judy the superior type of girl that she is, maybe there is something to it after all, he mused. And maybe it is as different from his own religion as Judy is from the other girls he knew, and she certainly is special. Danny decided to find out.

Chapter Two

IS THERE A GOD?

☐ Judy could hardly sleep that night. Danny's question really bothered her. She knew now that it was something she must discover for herself. Is there a living God? She could no longer take someone else's answer to that.

She remembered hearing her parents bear their testimonies in fast meeting. They seemed to know well enough, and she had always accepted their word on nearly everything. She would talk with them about Danny's question. She respected their word, but she wanted to know also for herself. How would she go about finding the answer?

She thought again of her own prayers and knew that many of them had been answered, and yet for the first time, now that Danny had raised the question, doubts began to enter her mind.

Were her answers to prayers actual answers after all? Did they come from God? Or were they but coincidences in her life?

Judy really began to worry now and decided to make a serious investigation of her own religion, so that she could know for herself whether the gospel were fact or fiction.

She decided to study as she had never studied before, and she would pray harder, too. She admitted to herself that her prayers were not much more than recitations of what she had learned and memorized as a little child.

She said them regularly enough, but that just about described them. She merely "said" them. She never had prayed earnestly about anything. No crisis had ever occurred in her life, nothing to worry much about, and nothing to bring her to the point of actually pleading with the Lord. She had never faced any particular opposition and had not felt any great need to pray. So she merely "said" her prayers.

Since she had grown up with prayers—at least with "saying" them—praying had been like any other part of

---

THE LORD'S SIDE

Who's on the Lord's side? Who?
Now is the time to show;
We ask it fearlessly,
Who's on the Lord's side? Who?
We serve the living God;
And want his foes to know
That if but few, we're great;
Who's on the Lord's side? Who?
—*Hymns*, No. 175

her daily routine, but with nothing to give it any depth.

As she thought about it now, she wondered if all of her teaching and thinking about the Church had not been rather superficial. There certainly had been nothing very soul stirring about it.

Then she remembered a lesson she had heard once in Sunday School. It came from the Book of Mormon. What was the name of that man in the lesson, and what did he do?

She went to a little bookcase in her room and took down the Book of Mormon. She looked at the chapter headings, hoping to recall that name. She thought she would like to read that episode again. It seemed to have a point of interest now, although it had not really impressed her when she first heard it.

It wasn't Nephi, she said, as she thumbed through the first two books. Nor was it Jacob. But was it Enos? That sounded more like it. She recalled that when she first heard that name she thought it sounded like Greek, and she wondered how a Greek name got into the Book of Mormon.

She saw that it was a short book of only one chapter, and she began to read it. She recognized it. This was what she wanted.

Like herself, Enos had been "raised in the church" and had often heard his parents talk about God. One day he also wanted to know for himself. As she glanced down the page, she read: "And I will tell you of the wrestle which I had before God."

She mused over that. This sounded like Jacob in the Bible.

"My soul hungered," she read on, "and I kneeled down before my Maker, and I cried unto him in mighty prayer and supplication."

She noted that he was troubled about sin, even as she now wondered about it. If she had yielded to Danny, she really would have been in sin. Fortunately she had not given in, but she wanted to know whether it would have been very wrong to "let herself go." That came back to the question Danny had raised: Is there a God?

Enos must have known that God lives or he would not have "wrestled" with him as he indicated. His soul "hungered." So did hers now. She certainly had developed a desire to know.

She read on.

". . . all the day long did I cry unto him; yea, and when night came I did still raise my voice high that it reached the heavens."

This helped her to understand what it meant to wrestle with the Lord.

"And there came a voice unto me, saying: Enos, thy sins are forgiven thee."

She paused for a moment and thought of Danny, and then read on:

"And I, Enos, knew that God could not lie; wherefore, my guilt was swept away."

God? Could not lie? Then Enos knew there was a God, and he heard his voice.

"And I said: Lord, how is it done?

"And he said unto me: Because of thy faith in Christ, whom thou hast never heard nor seen."

She continued to read: "I did pour out my whole soul unto God. . . . And while I was thus struggling in the spirit, behold, the voice of the Lord came into my mind again."

So it did take a struggle. It did take more than "saying prayers." A sense of peace and satisfaction now came to Judy. She was reassured by what Enos had said and done. She decided to struggle a little herself. She would begin to pray with this same sense of urgency that Enos mentioned, a hunger, both to pray and to study.

She was more determined now than ever before to find out if there is a God, for if he lives, there must be something also to the moral law which came from him. The two cannot be separated, she decided. If there is a God, his moral code must be lived or we cannot be at peace with him. Both she and Danny must come to understand that.

Chapter Three

CHARLES DARWIN & CO.

☐ Her biology class next day troubled her, so after school Judy went to the Institute of Religion to see Dr. Reeves, who always seemed to answer the questions troubling the other kids.

He was there and welcomed her. She told him about her biology class and asked why her professors always placed an atheistic interpretation on life and its beginning.

"It's true that many teachers do that," he said, "but it is their own opinions that they express for the most part. This is a tendency in school, I agree, but it does not represent the true spirit of science. Most of the great scientists are devout believers in God."

This startled and surprised Judy. It was certainly new to her. She had been so indoctrinated in her school career that she thought that atheism was about all the professors accepted.

Brother Reeves turned around and took from his desk a thick book entitled *The Descent of Man,* by Charles Darwin, the original evolutionist.

"Did you know that Darwin himself was a sincere believer in God?" he asked her. Of course she did not know. She had thought just the opposite. He turned to page 468 of his volume and read: "The question of whether there exists a Creator and Ruler of the Universe has been answered in the affirmative by some of the highest intellects that have ever existed."

"Let me see that book," Judy said, reaching to take it from Brother Reeves' hands.

She opened it to the title page, and there it was! *The Descent of Man* by Charles Darwin. It was a new edition of that old book, published in New York City by the Modern Library Press.

"This surprises me," she said. "I thought he was an atheist."

"No, he wasn't," Dr. Reeves explained. "He mistakenly dreamed up his theory of evolution, but it was only his own idea of how God created life. He did not exclude God. He merely assumed that this was God's method of creation."

"But surely it wasn't—or could it be?" she asked.

"No," continued Dr. Reeves. "The best-known scientists no longer believe that theory because they know now that the various species of life never change from one to another. The genes prevent any such changes. Mutations may come within species, but new species are never developed by the crossing of lines to alter the basic forms of life."

He looked into the puzzled eyes of Judy and smiled, then continued:

"In Genesis we read that God—in whom Darwin believed—decreed that all life must reproduce after its own kind. It is obvious that Darwin did not read his Bible very carefully, for he missed this vital point, that all life *must* reproduce after its own kind. To do otherwise would be to violate the decrees of the Almighty and would result in a mass of confusion.

"Judy, through archaeology we know that wheat in the days of ancient Egypt was precisely the same as wheat today. Corn is always corn. Cows are always cows. Horses are always horses. And human beings are always human beings. There are no missing links for any of these life forms.

"When efforts have been made to crossbreed animals of different species, nothing has resulted. Cows and horses cannot interbreed, for example. Nature has given them neither the inclination nor the power to do so. You can leave cows and horses in the same pasture indefinitely and they will never attempt to interbreed. It is not their nature, and they do not go against nature. Only man attempts that.

"The species do not change over the ages either. I went through the Field Museum of Natural History in Chicago and saw there an exhibit of the horseshoe crab. One specimen was strictly modern. Another next to it, placed there for the sake of comparison, was identical to it in every way. The identifying card said so. But the second one was listed as being 15 million years old. It was the identical crab species in both cases. The X ray proved that. This illustrates what I mean."

Dr. Reeves then turned to a newspaper on his desk, picked it up, and said, "Judy, you may not have seen today's paper. It has an article on this very subject."

He pointed to a news dispatch entitled "Adam and Eve vs. Darwin." Then he read from it. The dispatch said:

THIS I BELIEVE

Belief in God and in immortality thus gives us the moral strength and the ethical guidance we need for virtually every action in our daily life. Now in a modern world many people seem to feel that science has somehow made such religious ideas untimely or old-fashioned, but I think science has a real surprise for the skeptics. Science, for instance, tells us that nothing in nature, not even the tiniest particle, can disappear without a trace. Think about that for a moment. Once you do, your thoughts about life will never be the same. Nature does not know extinction. All it knows is transformation. Now if God applies this fundamental principle to the most minute and insignificant part of the universe, doesn't it make sense to assume that He applies it also to the masterpiece of His creation, the human soul? I think it does. And everything science has taught me and continues to teach me strengthens my belief in the continuity of our spiritual existence after death. Nothing can disappear without a trace.

—Dr. Werner von Braun
Space Authority

"Sacramento, California (UPI)—Spurning the pleas of the scientific community, the California Board of Education Thursday ordered the downgrading of Darwin's theory of evolution in public school textbooks.

"The decision was expected to have nationwide impact because several publishers plan to tailor texts used across the country to California's requirements because of the state's lucrative book market.

"After four hours of philosophical debate reminiscent of the famous Scopes 'monkey trial' of a half century ago, the board voted 7 to 1 to set textbook standards downgrading Darwin's theory on the origin of man to mere speculation."

"Note that," said Dr. Reeves. "Mere speculation. And that is what it is."

Dr. Reeves then quoted Dr. Walter Edward Lammerts of the University of California, a geneticist, as saying that "the science of genetics offers no evidence for belief in the two most basic assumptions of Charles Darwin. Except for occasional changes, the lines breed true and do not vary in all possible directions as postulated by Darwin."

Brother Reeves then asked, "At this point may I mention some modern scripture that fits into this discussion? It is very interesting to me."

He opened his Doctrine and Covenants to section 77 and mentioned to Judy that the Prophet Joseph, like other people, found the book of Revelation in the Bible difficult to understand. Therefore, he asked the Lord for some explanations and received them by revelation.

"Let me read to you now:

" 'Q. What are we to understand by the four beasts, spoken of in the same verse?

" 'A. They are figurative expressions used by the Revelator, John, in describing heaven, the paradise of God, the happiness of man, and of beasts, and of creeping things, and of the fowls of the air; that which is spiritual being in the likeness of that which is temporal; and that which is temporal in the likeness of that which is spiritual. . . .' "

Here Brother Reeves paused for a moment. "Note these next words, Judy, if you will. They are most significant: 'the spirit of man in the likeness of his person, as also the spirit of the beast, and every other creature which God has created.' "

This left Judy open-eyed and wondering.

"But what does it mean?" she asked.

Brother Reeves then turned to the Book of Moses in the Pearl of Great Price, where the story of the creation is told. He read from the third chapter of Moses, where the Lord says:

"And now, behold, I say unto you, that these are the generations of the heaven and of the earth, when they were created in the day that I, the Lord God, made the heaven and the earth;

"And every plant of the field before it was in the earth, and every herb of the field before it grew. For I, the Lord God, created all things, of which I have spoken, spiritually, before they were naturally upon the face of the earth . . . for in heaven created I them. . . ."

"Do you understand now, Judy?" he asked.

He took his Bible next and turned to Genesis, second chapter, beginning with verse 4:

"These are the generations of the heavens and of the earth when they were created, in the day that the Lord God made the earth and the heavens,

"And every plant of the field, before it was in the earth, and every herb of the field before it grew. . . ."

"You see," he went on, "there were two creations. In the first one, all things were made as spirits. You know that we human beings are spirits, and that we lived as such before we were born. We Latter-day Saints accept this, don't we, Judy? The scriptures support that fact.

"The animals and birds and all other forms of life were created as spirits also. Then in the second creation, God provided mortal bodies for all forms of life, and the spirits of animals, birds, trees, and human beings were placed within those bodies.

"To come back to section 77 of the Doctrine and Covenants, the spirit and body resemble each other, 'that which is temporal in the likeness of that which is spiritual; the spirit of man in the likeness of his person, as also the spirit of the beast, and every other creature which God has created.'

"This," Dr. Reeves went on, "demonstrates that there could not be mutations from one species to another.

"The body is in the likeness of the spirit. The spirit was made before the earth. There were spirits of dogs and cats and cows and horses and birds and bees. In mortality they were given bodies to match their spirits, just as we were.

"Since the spirits were created before the earth, and since the bodies were to be in the likeness of the spirits, there could be no mutations on earth, for the body had to follow the pattern or design or the form of the spirit.

"So birds were birds from the beginning—even in the spirit. Monkeys and men were monkeys and men from the beginning—even in the spirit. There could be no missing links between them.

"This explains why God said in Genesis that everything was to reproduce after its own kind. They had to so that the mortal body would match the spirit, whether in bird or beast or man.

"Would God allow for any confusion? Would he allow the spirit of a man to enter the body of an ape? Would he allow the spirit of a horse to enter the body of a cow?

When we understand the doctrine behind the creation, we can see why there could not be mutations such as Darwin described. We can also see how and why God made interbreeding impossible between species, for otherwise there would be nothing but confusion.

"Human beings can only reproduce as human beings. Cows can only bring forth cows. To be facetious, I am sure that you never have heard of a cow having a colt or a horse having a calf, have you?

"No, Judy, there is no such thing as evolution as Darwin described it. We can have mutations, surely enough, within the species, such as breeding different strains of dogs, for example, but never crossing species. Again to be facetious, dogs and cats could never interbreed, much as the dogs like to chase after cats.

"And what does all this prove? That there is an intelligent God who created all things and knew what he was about when he did so."

Judy then thought to herself, *And he also knew what he was about when he gave us the moral law.*

"Just one further point, Judy," said Dr. Reeves. "You note that everything reproduces after its own kind. This includes God himself, so that his spirit children resemble him in form. That is why the scripture says that man is in the image and likeness of God. It could be in no other way."

Chapter Four

FROM
OUTER
SPACE

☐ Dr. Reeves spent another hour with Judy, reviewing the works of prominent scientists, Mormon and non-Mormon, all of them testifying to their belief in God. He mentioned some who felt that their discoveries in the field of science actually came as inspiration from "outer space."

He quoted Dr. Alfred G. Fisk of San Francisco State College, author of *The Search for Life's Meaning,* who said:

"The scientists frequently speak of new insights coming to them like bolts out of the blue, from without. Our common word referring to new scientific truth is 'discovery,' implying that what is discovered is already there, objective, not a creation of the mind of the observer. . . . They must be revelations from a supra-human mind or person."

At one time Fritz Kreisler, the great violinist, spoke

of the same kind of experience coming to him as he played his beautiful instrument. Kreisler said, "Whenever I am lifted out of the material plane and come in touch with another, a holier world, it is as if some hand other than my own were directing the bow over the strings."

When Haydn composed the glorious oratorio *The Creation,* he said, "Not from me, but from above it all has come." Handel said a similar thing about his composing the *Messiah.* He wrote it in a remarkably short time, as if by dictation from above, which he actually thought it was.

Judy walked away from the institute building that afternoon with an entirely new conception of things. Her faith was regenerated. If those intelligent men mentioned by Dr. Reeves believed so firmly in God, who was she to doubt him?

Brother Reeves had urged her to read the revelations of God to his prophets, modern and ancient, for they were men who actually saw God and talked with him. Revelation, he had said, is far more convincing than science.

She did as he suggested and was especially thrilled with the testimony of the Prophet Joseph Smith as she read it over and over again. His first vision was certainly a marvelous experience As she read it, she felt within herself a conviction that it was true. How could she doubt it?

And since it was so impressive, should she not also accept his teachings, even in the matter of personal conduct?

She was fascinated by the testimony of Joseph Smith and Sidney Rigdon as given in the 76th section of the Doctrine and Covenants. It seemed to sweep all doubts from her mind:

". . . this is the testimony, last of all, which we give of him: That he lives!

"For we saw him, even on the right hand of God; and

we heard the voice bearing record that he is the Only Begotten of the Father—

"That by him, and through him, and of him, the worlds are and were created. . . ."

She believed. Tears trickled down her cheeks as the testimony came to her. A warmth swept over her entire system. She knew beyond words that God lives.

She determined to read the scriptures and find out more about him. It could only be through revelation that she could really come to know him—revelation and her own prayers. She would read the revelations given to the prophets, and she would pray, she thought, like Enos. Each time she knelt before her Heavenly Father now, she thought of him.

But it was not a struggle for her to pray as it had been for Enos. With what she had learned from Brother Reeves, and from her own scriptural reading, she now prayed with calm assurance about God. Actually, as she prayed, she felt a deep satisfaction that she had never experienced before.

She felt now that she could answer Danny's question. She was fully satisfied in her own mind. Yes, there is a God.

But this conviction brought back the matter that had raised the question in the first place, God and his laws on morality.

There was no point, she said to herself, in believing in God unless she lived what he taught. Otherwise she would be a hypocrite, and she remembered that the Lord condemned hypocrisy.

Believing in God meant believing also in Jesus Christ, the Savior. She remembered that he had said some things about morality in the Sermon on the Mount. What were they?

She turned to the book of Matthew and began to read that greatest of all sermons.

"Ye have heard that it was said by them of old time, Thou shalt not commit adultery." She paused, and recalled that this was one of the Ten Commandments, and they were given by God. He certainly did not give them unless he intended that they should be obeyed.

She read on:

"But I say unto you that whosoever looketh on a woman to lust after her hath committed adultery with her already in his heart."

She paused over this. Moses had taught that the act of adultery was to be punished by death in his day. Now Jesus said that it was evil even to look upon another person with lust.

She thought now of Danny. When he had tried so hard to break down her resistance, did he have anything but lust in his heart? He just wanted to make a plaything of her, she was sure of that. He merely wanted to stir up his own passions by improper approaches, and certainly that was lustful. And if she had allowed petting, as he wanted, how much farther would he have gone?

Then she started to think about petting. Jesus must have had this in mind, although he did not use that word. It is a rather modern expression.

But if the Savior condemned merely looking on another with lust, what would he have said about touching, and fondling, and petting?

She shuddered at the thought of Danny's evil approach. He wanted to have fun at her expense, and at what cost it would have been—loss of self-respect, loss of his respect for her, a breakdown of her character, making herself cheap and common. She would have hated herself for the rest of her life, now that she understood a little more about her religion and what it taught.

The Savior talked about this same thing when he gave the Sermon on the Mount to the Nephites, only he added a little. She turned now to the twelfth chapter of Third Nephi and read:

"I say unto you, that whosoever looketh on a woman, to lust after her, hath committed adultery already in his heart.

"Behold, I give unto you a commandment, that ye suffer none of these things to enter into your heart.

"For it is better that ye should deny yourselves of these things, wherein ye will take up your cross, than that ye should be cast into hell."

He said we should not allow such thoughts even to enter our minds.

She remembered what President McKay had taught:

First a thought,
Then an act.

She could understand the Savior's words better now. And certainly if we do not allow the thoughts of evil to enter our minds, we will not commit the act.

So even the *thought* of lust was condemned by the Lord.

What else had the Savior taught on this subject? She was determined that if she was going to believe in him, she would follow his teachings, and since sex was given so much publicity these days, she had better learn all she could about the Lord's view on the subject.

She found section 42 in the Doctrine and Covenants. There was what seemed to be a restatement of some of the Ten Commandments. It spoke of morality too.

She read this, as given by Jesus to Joseph Smith:

"He that looketh upon a woman to lust after her shall deny the faith, and shall not have the Spirit; and if he repents not he shall be cast out.

"Thou shalt not commit adultery; and he that committeth adultery, and repenteth not, shall be cast out.

"But he that has committed adultery and repents with all his heart, and forsaketh it, and doeth it no more, thou shalt forgive."

That shed more light on the subject. She supposed that being "cast out" meant being excommunicated from the Church. There was repentance, and forgiveness through sincere repentance. "But," she continued to read, "if he doeth it again, he shall not be forgiven, but shall be cast out."

Of course Danny did not know about this. He did not even belong to our church, she said to herself, but whether in the Church or out of the Church, the Lord had spoken, and it applies to everyone.

How thrilled she was that she had not given in to Danny!

Chapter Five

THE
REASONS
WHY

☐ Judy now began to wonder just what was the thinking behind these laws. Why was God so strict in this matter? What was his reasoning?

She went back to Brother Reeves, and he taught her some of the great basics of our religion.

"No one can understand sex," he said, "without first understanding our relationship to God, for he made sex and provided for its use, not only in the human family, but in lower forms as well. It was his plan, his method of perpetuating the race. And he pronounced his creative plans good.

"We must understand," continued Brother Reeves, "that we are the family of God. He does have a family, just as we have families here in mortality. We belong to his family. We are his children, his actual offspring."

He turned now to the seventeenth chapter of Acts in the New Testament and read from Paul, who taught the Greeks that we are truly the children of God, his literal offspring.

"But what does that mean?" asked Judy. "How can we be the offspring of God when we are the offspring of our mortal parents here on earth?"

"That is a logical question," replied the institute teacher. "And it must be answered. We are really dual beings."

"And that means what?" she queried.

"Do you recall our discussion when you were here last time, and we said that all life was made in heaven before it was placed here on earth? Everything has a spirit. The animals have spirits, the birds have spirits, and we have spirits.

"But there is a great difference between them and us. They were creations of God—that is, he made them, designed them, fashioned them, and gave them life.

"It was not so with us, however, for we came into existence by birth. He is the Father of our spirits as our fathers in mortality provided us with our mortal bodies."

"And what about our mothers?" she asked.

"Do you recall our favorite hymn, 'O My Father,' written by Eliza R. Snow? Just think about these words in that song:

'In the heavens are parents single?
No; the thought makes reason stare!
Truth is reason, truth eternal
Tells me I've a mother there.'

"You know about temple marriage in the Church, don't you, Judy? That allows us to go on as married couples in the world to come and there continue to be parents—only of spirits.

"It is this way in which God became the Father of our

spirits. This is the beauty of our great religion. We believe in eternal progression, but that progression is based on family life. We shall continue—throughout eternity—to reproduce ourselves, if we obey his laws.

"This is what God is doing, and this is how we became his children. There is an old saying in the Church that goes like this:

'As man is, God once was.

As God is, man may become.'

"This is credited to President Lorenzo Snow, the fourth president of our church.

"You recall that the Savior commanded in the Sermon on the Mount that we should become perfect, even as our Father which is in heaven is perfect. Do you see now how this may be realized?

"Then can you understand about our being the literal offspring of God in the spirit? We are spirits. God is a spirit also, but he is embodied in an eternal body of flesh and bone, such as we will have after our resurrection.

"But we were born to him as spirits. Therefore, we really are a part of God and resemble him in form. We have divinity within us. As we now are flesh after the flesh of our earthly parents, and are truly a part of them, so we have a portion of God within us, since we are his spirit offspring.

"Our bodies are houses in which our spirits live. The scripture refers to our bodies as the temples of God. That is easy to understand, isn't it? Our bodies house the offspring of God, a part of God, meaning our spirit selves.

"Think of the temples we build here on earth. Do you recall the temple in Jerusalem, which Jesus cleansed? The people there sold sheep, oxen, and birds to be used as sacrifices on the altars of the temple in those days. But they actually brought the animals into the temple to sell them. They had their money tables inside the temple and

AND HERE IS LIGHT

The doctrine of the pre-existence—revealed so plainly, particularly in latter days—pours a wonderful flood of light upon the otherwise mysterious problem of man's origin. It shows that man, as a spirit, was begotten and born of heavenly parents, and reared to maturity in the eternal mansions of the Father, prior to coming upon the earth, in a temporal body to undergo experience in mortality. It teaches that all men existed in the spirit before any man existed in the flesh, and that all who had inhabited the earth since Adam had taken bodies and become souls in like manner.

It is held by some that Adam was not the first man upon this earth, and that the original human was a development from lower orders of the animal creation. These, however, are the theories of men. The word of the Lord declares that Adam was "the first man of all men" (Moses 1:34) and we are therefore in duty bound to regard him as the primal parent of our race.

—The First Presidency
Joseph F. Smith
John R. Winder
Anthon H. Lund

transacted business there, selling sacrifices to people who wanted to offer them on the altar.

"This angered the Savior, and so he drove them out. He cleansed the temple.

"Think for a moment of our beautiful temples. Can you imagine them being invaded by sheep and cows and money changers who would sell animals to people coming there? It is unthinkable, of course.

"It would be sacrilegious also for anyone to bring cows and sheep into our ward chapels and use them for barns. They would defile these sacred buildings, wouldn't they?

"Then what about the temples of our bodies? Are not our bodies, which house a part of God—our spirits—more sacred than any structure made of stone and wood?

"Then shouldn't they be kept as clean and pure?

"And why are they to be kept so clean and pure? Because in God's great plan, these bodies will make more bodies for more of his spirits who are to come to earth as we have come, and they should be kept pure and clean for that purpose.

"Our bodies are essential to our eternal progression. They deserve a clean beginning, a respectable birth and parentage. We will take these bodies—these same bodies which we now have—into the resurrection, and on into eternity. Will we be proud of them?

"Think for a moment about the significance of it all. How would you like to take into eternity a body that had been besmirched with sin? It would be a terrible reminder of an evil life, wouldn't it?

"But think in another direction. When we have children, should they not be entitled to a clean and honorable birth? Whether children are born through evil means or through honorable marriage, they will still be our children. Nothing can change that.

"What kind of recollections will we want to carry with us about their conception and birth, through both this life and the next?

"We are commanded to become like God. In other words, we are expected to become like our Father in his family life, his eternal family life.

"We are his representatives in bringing new life into this world. Knowing what it all means, dare we bring new life into this world in any way other than the Lord's way, which is through clean and wholesome procreation within legal marriage?

"God has given the power of procreation to all forms of life. As we said, everything is to bring forth after its own kind.

"There is no marriage among the lower forms of life, because God controls their procreation otherwise. But *we* are the offspring and children of God, and we are to become like him.

"Therefore, for us, procreation must come only in his way—never outside of marriage, never as a part of lust, never in an effort to make the sex act a means of entertainment. Always it must be in righteousness as God would have it. We must forever remember who we are, and why we have sex, and then act accordingly, as President David O. McKay used to say.

"So Judy, that is the reasoning behind chastity. And it makes good sense, doesn't it?"

THE HAPPIEST PEOPLE

The happiest people I have known have not been the men of great worldly achievements, or of accomplishments, or of wealth. They have been the simple people who are happily married, enjoying good health and good family life. Success in the generally accepted sense of the term means the opportunity to experience and to realize to the maximum the forces that are within you.

> —Dr. David Sarnoff
> Chairman of the Board
> Radio Corporation of
> America (RCA)

Chapter Six

CHASTITY

IS

DIVINE

☐ A student assembly was planned for all institute students. Judy expected to attend. One of the General Authorities was to be the speaker, and it was assured that there would be a large attendance.

As Judy walked into the hall she was surprised to see Danny there too. She did not know that he was making an investigation of the Church. Her resistance on the night of their date had wakened him to a new sense of decency. He now wanted to know more.

Judy avoided him and sat on the opposite side of the hall. She was in no mood to resume the argument they had had in his car.

The chapel at the institute was packed with students. The lecture had been widely advertised on campus. Many were anxious to hear the talk about chastity, which was to be the subject of the discussion.

The meeting began with some songs from the institute choir. Fred Warburton offered the opening prayer, and Brother Reeves introduced the speaker, who greeted the audience and complimented them highly on their allegiance to the Church.

He said that the young people of today are the finest generation the Lord has yet sent to the earth, at least in our time. And he said that this generation has a great destiny to fulfill in helping to build the kingdom of God in preparation for the second coming of Christ.

He said to them:

I am grateful for your faith in God and in his Son Jesus Christ. As you know, God, through his Beloved Son, created this and all other worlds.

The scriptures say that all things were made by him, and without him was not anything made that was made. (John 1.)

He made the earth and the sea, and all forms of life. As he did so, he commanded each form of life to reproduce in its own sphere; that is, each species was to reproduce after its own kind.

Reproduction, then, was part of God's plan. Without it, life could not be perpetuated in the animal, vegetable, or human spheres.

God made sex as the means by which reproduction was to be achieved. So he commanded all forms of life to function in their sex to bring about this reproduction.

When he had finished his creation, he called it good. Note that God made sex, and he pronounced it good.

Then he brought Adam and Eve into the world. Their coming was different from the creation of all other life. As you know, all forms of life were created in the spirit before they were in their mortal forms.

We each have a spirit, which came from our preexistence. Our bodies were provided here as houses or temples for our spirits to live in. This was true of all forms of life.

Although God made all other forms of life both in the spirit for the preexistence and in the flesh for mortality, it was not so with Adam and Eve. They were not creations in the literal sense.

All human beings lived in the preexistence with God, and all were his spirit offspring. In other words, each of us is a child of God; our spirits, which inhabit our bodies, are our real individual selves, and as such we are God's children—his offspring, as Paul expressed it.

When he placed Adam and Eve on the earth he thereby introduced his own offspring into the world, and he expected that Adam and Eve would provide bodies for their children, and thus procreation would begin for all human beings on the earth.

The Lord placed safeguards about reproduction among the lower forms of life. For instance, he required that each of the species would reproduce only within its own sphere. There would be no crossing of species. For example, cows would always be cows, and horses would always by horses, but cows and horses could not interbreed. That would bring confusion. God realized this and therefore restricted this reproduction to the individual species. The scripture uses the expression "after its own kind" in each instance. And again he pronounced it good.

Reproduction among the lower forms was also limited to certain seasons or periods of time, and no effort at reproduction was made at other times.

Reproduction among humans was different, however, because humans were of a higher order. They were the children of God.

Lower forms were not given any moral laws. Their instincts and natural restrictions took care of the need.

However, with man, it was different.

God gave to human beings their free agency; he gave them a knowledge of good and evil, and moral laws to help them choose between good and evil.

Next he introduced the institution of marriage. He gave Eve to Adam in the holy bonds of matrimony.

Then, and not until then, did he command them to reproduce themselves.

Note this carefully:

1. They were his spirit children, and could become like him if they would obey him.

2. They were given their right of choice, which we call free agency.

3. They were given a moral law to help them understand and choose that which is right.

4. They were given marriage.

Only under these conditions were they to reproduce.

When the Lord had completed his creation of the human race, had given them their agency, the moral law, and matrimony, and had commanded them under these conditions to multiply and replenish the earth, he pronounced it all very good.

You see, then, that God made sex, and it was very good for his purpose, which was that of reproduction. It was essential or otherwise the race would die out.

He placed strong restrictions about reproduction by the human race, because he wanted to keep it "very good." It was sacred. It was part of the divine plan. It was part of God's work of creation, and mankind in this respect became partners with God in his creative effort.

It was all very good. But it must be kept that way. It must always be regarded as being sacred.

But the devil had other ideas. He had attempted to destroy the plan of salvation in the preexistent life and had failed. Now he sought to fight God by destroying the morals of his children. He went among Adam's family saying, "Believe it not," and many of them no longer believed in God.

The devil had introduced murder into the world by telling Cain that he could commit this crime and get gain. Obeying the devil, Cain killed Abel in the hope of obtaining his brother's property.

But God judged Cain immediately, and instead of gaining by his crime, Cain became the most miserable person on earth. But the devil was pleased with Cain's sin.

Satan stays with one theme: sin to get gain. He has done so all through the centuries. As he went among Adam's children, telling them not to believe the gospel teachings, he introduced immorality, and as a result adulterous living became so common that eventually the Lord had to destroy all life on earth in the flood of Noah's day.

Satan is doing the same thing today. He is telling you and me and every other human being that it is no sin to indulge in illicit sex—"let yourself go," to use the modern expression—and in doing so he makes his temptation very glamorous and alluring.

One of the immediate means by which he destroys morality is through his attack on modesty of dress.

His philosophy is that the human body is beautiful, and to be appreciated it should be seen. He knows very well that exposure of the human form, and particularly of the feminine form, becomes a temptation to commit adultery. So he attacks modesty.

How is it expressed in our day? Through the miniskirts, the "hot pants," the low necks, the strapless evening gowns, the tight sweaters that are so form-revealing, skimpy bathing suits, and now topless and bottomless styles on beaches and in theaters and night clubs.

The present emphasis upon sex in movies, on the radio, in books and magazines, and even on billboards is but an expression of his effort to destroy virtue. It seems that wherever one turns there is sex appeal.

But notice that it is not an emphasis that would glorify sex in righteousness; it does not build up the sanctity of the home, nor does it picture motherhood as something sacred.

The entire emphasis is on the illicit side. He would destroy virtue and fidelity of husband and wife, establish promiscuity among youth, and do anything to make sex common and cheap. He seeks to rob it of its high and sacred position as provided by the Lord in creation.

Since the sanctity of the body is so related to the sanctity of sex, why make the body common? Why expose to the public eye this sacred thing which is the temple of God? Girls, when you expose your bodies, you do yourselves a great injustice, and you likewise do your boyfriends an injury.

If only you girls could sit behind a curtain sometimes when we have private interviews with boys and hear these boys really express themselves, man to man, about how they feel concerning modesty in dress! Many of them have said that their moral downfall began with a girl's immodest dress. Some were tempted, on the dance floor, by bosoms that were not properly covered.

And then Satan carries it further. After he breaks down modesty, he moves into such things as petting parties. Will you mind if I speak frankly about petting?

A lovely girl came into my office within the week and said, "I wish you would tell me what the Church thinks about petting."

I said, "Do you pet?"

"Yes, I do, and that's why I'm wondering about it. Sometimes we pet rather heavily."

When you pet, what do you do? I know there's necking and I know there's kissing, but in "heavy" petting you expose your bodies to the other person, don't you? Boy or girl. Lovely girls allow boys to handle and stimulate their bodies in a petting party, and even encourage it, sometimes. Occasionally girls handle the bodies of boys and stimulate them. What goes on in their minds in a situation of that kind? Is there anything "virtuous or lovely or of good report, or praiseworthy" about a party of that kind?

The Savior said: ". . . whosoever looketh on a woman to lust after her hath committed adultery with her already in his heart." (Matt. 5:28.)

Think that over in terms of petting.

He said in modern revelation, ". . . he that looketh upon a woman to lust after her shall deny the faith, and shall not have the Spirit; and if he repents not he shall be cast out." (D&C 42:23.)

Think of that in terms of petting.

When people engage in heavy petting, is there anything but lust in the mind? ". . . whosoever looketh on a woman to lust after her hath committed adultery with her already in his heart."

The Savior did not in these words actually refer to the sexual embrace. He said, ". . . whosoever *looketh* on a woman to lust after her."

But the man who not only looketh upon her but handles her as well—does he lust after her? And if he does, he has committed adultery with her in his heart, according to the Son of God.

Is it serious, this petting? Can you lose your chastity piecemeal? Can you? Can you lose your money a dollar at a time?

If you, as a young lady, get in an automobile and allow a boy to handle your body, and you possibly handle his, are you losing any of your virtue?

Does any man have the right to touch the body of a woman to whom he is not married?

We do lose our chastity piecemeal, and when young people engage in petting, they then lose a portion of their virtue; not the complete loss, until they go all the way, but they partially lose their chastity in petting.

Can you interpret it in any other way in the light of the words of the Savior? ". . . whosoever looketh on a woman to lust after her hath committed adultery with her already in his heart."

Petting is a step, and almost a final step, toward complete loss of virtue. And that is what Satan is leading up to. He knows that sex is sacred. And he is determined to prostitute it wherever and whenever he can.

IS IT "REALISM"?

Can anyone deny that movies are dirtier than ever? But they don't call it dirt. They call it "realism." Why do we let them fool us? Why do we nod owlishly when they tell us that filth is merely a daring art form, that licentiousness is really social comment? Isn't it plain that the financially harassed movie industry is putting gobs of sex in the darkened drive-ins in an effort to lure curious teenagers away from their TV sets? Last week the screen industry solemnly announced that henceforth perversion and homosexuality would no longer be barred from the screen provided the subjects were handled with "delicacy and taste." Good heavens!

—Jenkin Lloyd Jones
(From an address to the American
Society of Newspaper Editors)

Oh, if you could listen to some of the heartbroken confessions from girls and boys who thought they were having fun and who later find out that instead they have brought the wrath of God on themselves and have committed a crime next to murder in its seriousness!

What is your destiny? As a child of God, as one of the race of the Gods, you have as your destiny the great opportunity of becoming like him sometime. But only those who prove themselves will ever reach that goal.

Serious as sex sin is, much as we must avoid it, if by some chance any of you have fallen, the Lord does hold out this hope: that if you will now do what is right, God will forgive. Let me read some of what he says on this general subject:

"Thou shalt love thy wife with all thy heart, and shalt cleave unto her and none else.

"And he that looketh upon a woman to lust after her shall deny the faith, and shall not have the Spirit; and if he repents not he shall be cast out.

"Thou shalt not commit adultery; and he that committeth adultery, and repenteth not, shall be cast out."

That means excommunication as far as the Church is concerned; and so far as the Lord is concerned, they shall be cast out of heaven.

"But he that has committed adultery and repents with all his heart, and forsaketh it, and doeth it no more, thou shalt forgive;

"But if he doeth it again, he shall not be forgiven, but shall be cast out." (D&C 42:22-26.)

In the Bible, there is a chapter in Ezekiel that is also on this subject—chapter 18. There the Lord says that if the person who has sinned will now turn from all his transgressions and do them no more, never returning to them, and for the rest of his life keep the commandments of

God, the Lord will forgive him and will never mention his sins to him again.

In the 58th section of the Doctrine and Covenants, verses 42 and 43, the Lord says something similar, explaining that if we fully repent and then serve him, he will not only forgive our sins, but will also forget them. In other words, he will not mention them to us again.

This is a marvelous promise and shows the great mercy of God, who desires only that we reform our lives and serve him so that eventually we may become like him. But he knows, and we know, that if we fail to serve him, we cannot become like him.

It is always worse to sin against the light than to sin in ignorance. Therefore, all of you who have kept yourselves clean thus far and who now know the facts about chastity must continue to keep yourselves pure and virtuous. You have the truth. Do not sin against it.

Not one of you would purposely stain your clothing for a supposed thrill, not fearing to do so because you know there is a cleaning company around the corner that would eliminate the stains.

It is even more senseless to stain your soul, while knowing what it means. To deliberately sin against the light, hoping that later repentance would bring forgiveness, would be folly indeed.

Is not God intelligent? Would he not know what you were doing? You would be trying to live on both sides of the fence at the same time, and this is hypocrisy, a thing that God denounces. Do not commit sin with any such foolish notion in mind.

In its truest sense, parenthood is next to Godhood, because fathers and mothers who serve the Lord participate with him in his creative plan.

But parenthood is good only when sex is used under

the restrictions and regulations that the Lord provided for it. Otherwise procreation becomes evil.

The use of sex is ordained of God only in legal marriage. If we marry properly in the temple, then our parenthood may be projected into the eternities, as God has designed.

Can you see then why Satan tries to corrupt sex? It is one of his ways of keeping you out of the celestial kingdom of God.

May we be true and virtuous, remembering that virtue is more important than life. Protect it above your life. If the time ever comes that you must choose between the two, then sacrifice your life, but under no circumstances sacrifice your virtue.

If you die clean, God will accept you, but no unclean thing can come into his presence.

```
┌─────────────────────────────────┐
│                                 │
│                                 │
│          PETTING                │
│                                 │
│             IS                  │
│                                 │
│            EVIL                 │
│                                 │
│                                 │
└─────────────────────────────────┘
```

☐ Judy learned that the lecture at the institute was only one of a series. Another was to be given on the following Tuesday as part of the MIA gathering. She attended. The same speaker was there and said this:

Let us understand each other clearly. Petting is, in and of itself, an immoral act. But it also often leads to a complete loss of virtue.

Some have told us, as they have confessed their sins, that they had no intention of going so far, that they had always promised themselves they would protect their virtue, but things got out of hand. Too much "loving" swept matters out of control so fast they hardly realized what they were doing.

It is like taking the first drink or the first cigarette. If we did not take the first and initial step, we would not take the subsequent ones. We must avoid the very appearance of evil.

Now once the evil act is committed, what problems arise? They are many.

In the first place, there is the matter of whether or not it can be kept a secret. We must admit the fact in the first place. It cannot be kept hidden. Girls, you must realize that boys do talk, sometimes boastfully advertising to their boy friends how far they went with a certain date one night.

Often it becomes locker-room gossip, then a subject of joking. The boys laugh about it, ridicule and make fun of the girl who had no more self-respect than to allow a boy to paw her, and pet her, and humble her.

And boys, don't you think that all the girls keep a secret either. Many of them talk too, and their talk is far from flattering to you.

But there is another phase of the subject. What about telling mother and dad? You say it would nearly kill them. So it would. But in a time like that, they of all people should know. They are your best friends. They will help you more than any other persons.

So before you commit the contemplated sin, ask yourself how you are going to break the news to your folks who love you so much.

And then there is your bishop. He must know too, and in the normal course of events he will find out. Think about the way you will approach him; think about it seriously before you commit that act which will make this confession necessary. Remember that adultery, like murder, will sometime be brought into the open.

But don't make your confession to inexperienced persons or to your young friends. Because of their inexperience they may mislead you. Get good counsel. It may be had as easily as bad counsel. And don't keep your problem on your mind and worry about it all by yourself, breaking down your nerves and your general health. Be wise. Go to your parents, and go to your bishop, and make the wise and necessary adjustment.

Then there is the possibility of a child, the sweet innocent victim of a dreadful sin. What should be done about him? An operation, some may suggest, but is that really a way out? Would not that be jumping from the frying pan into the fire? Shall we compound our sin with further and probably much worse sin?

Some states of the United States and many foreign countries have legalized abortion. But does that make it right?

No matter how we look at it, abortion is the destruction of life, and the Lord has commanded that we shall not kill.

In the 59th section of the Doctrine and Covenants we read: "Thou shalt not steal, neither commit adultery, nor kill, nor do anything like unto it."

In condemning abortion, the First Presidency, President Harold B. Lee, President N. Eldon Tanner, and President Marion G. Romney, recently issued the following statement on this subject:

"In view of a recent decision of the United States Supreme Court, we feel it necessary to restate the position of the church on abortion in order that there be no misunderstanding of our attitude.

"The church opposes abortion and counsels its members not to submit to or perform an abortion except in the rare cases where, in the opinion of competent medical counsel, the life or good health of the mother is seriously endangered or where the pregnancy was caused by rape and produces serious emotional trauma in the mother. Even then it should be done only after counseling with the local presiding priesthood authority and after receiving divine confirmation through prayer.

"Abortion must be considered one of the most revolting and sinful practices in this day, when we are witnessing the frightening evidence of permissiveness leading to sexual immorality.

"Members of the church guilty of being parties to the sin of abortion must be subjected to the disciplinary action of the councils of the church as circumstances warrant. In dealing with this serious matter, it would be well to keep in mind the word of the Lord stated in the 59th Section of the Doctrine of Covenants, verse 6, 'Thou shalt not steal; neither commit adultery, nor kill, nor do anything like unto it.'

"As to the amenability of the sin of abortion to the laws of repentance and forgiveness, we quote the following statement made by President David O. McKay and his counselors, Stephen L Richards and J. Reuben Clark Jr., which continues to represent the attitude and position of the church:

" 'As the matter stands today, no definite statement has been made by the Lord one way or another regarding the crime of abortion. So far as is known, He has not listed it alongside the crime of the unpardonable sin and shedding of innocent human blood. That He has not done so would suggest that it is not in that class of crime and therefore that it will be amenable to the laws of repentance and forgiveness.'

"This quoted statement, however, should not, in any sense, be construed to minimize the seriousness of this revolting sin."

Faced with the dilemma of an unwanted child, some girls are told to give the child away. But what can tear at the heartstrings of a mother more than that—a mother who has anticipated the birth of her child?

The Savior said of little children: "Take heed that ye despise not one of these little ones; for I say unto you, That in heaven their angels do always behold the face of my Father which is in heaven." (Matt. 18:10.)

But to keep the child out of wedlock raises serious problems, too. Will we have the courage to bring this unwanted illegitimate child to our family and friends, and let it be an admission of our guilt before all mankind?

WE HAVE REACHED THE POINT

We have reached the stomach-turning point. We have reached the point where we should reexamine the debilitating philosophy of permissiveness. Let this not be confused with the philosophy of liberty.

The school system that permits our children to develop a quarter of their natural talents is not a champion of our liberties. The healthy man who chooses to loaf on unemployment compensation is not a defender of human freedom. The playwright who would degrade us, the author who would profit from pandering to the worst that's in us, are no friends of ours.

It's time we hit the sawdust trail. It's time we revived the idea that there is such a thing as sin—just plain old willful sin. It is time we brought self-discipline back into style. And who has a greater responsibility at this hour than we?

—Jenkin Lloyd Jones
(From an address to the American Society of Newspaper Editors)

The wages of sin are multiplied every way we turn, and we wonder why we ever brought it upon ourselves. Was the momentary and very questionable thrill worth all this heartbreak and trouble? The price of sin is more than any of us can afford.

So, as Paul said to the Romans, "Let not sin therefore reign in your mortal body, that ye should obey it in the lusts thereof. Neither yield ye your members as instruments of unrighteousness unto sin: but yield yourselves unto God. . . ." (Rom. 6:12-13.)

I once heard a chorus of a hundred Primary children sing "My Body Is a Temple." As I listened, I turned and looked on their lovely faces and thought I understood a little better the words of the Master: ". . . of such is the kingdom of God." (Mark 10:14.)

Then I remembered another passage of scripture, this time from Nephi of old, who wrote: "I, Nephi, having been born of goodly parents. . . ." (1 Ne. 1:1.)

I looked again at those little children singing so beautifully that sacred song: "My Body Is a Temple."

Then I looked at the adult audience made up in large measure by the parents of those children. Nephi's words kept ringing in my ears: ". . . born of goodly parents. . . ."

Then I said to myself, every child should be born of goodly parents. Every child has the right to be wellborn. Every child has the right to know and bear the names— the true names—of his parents, and to be proud to do so —proud and thankful!

The world puts a high premium on legitimate things. It has only disdain for the illegitimate.

"My body is a temple!"

As a child, every human being has the right to be born with a body clean enough, and free enough from stain, to be a temple for the Spirit of God.

And every parent must keep his or her own body so

clean and so pure and so holy that it will be a temple, one fit to give birth in holiness to other temples in compliance with the laws of God which govern such births.

To quote Paul again: "Know ye not that your bodies are the members of Christ? shall I then take the members of Christ, and make them members of an harlot? God forbid." (1 Cor. 6:15.)

If we so live as to be fully worthy, it is the decree of the Lord that we may bring our body-temples back into his presence. But only those preserved in purity by holiness of life, and those which have been cleansed by the blood of Christ after sincere repentance, can be given this blessing. Worlds without end, the unclean which remains unclean, but which will also be resurrected, shall be forever incompatible with heavenly things.

For the pure and holy, a promise is made by the Lord that we may take part in a glorious resurrection. Our bodies—those in which we now live—then will be fashioned after the Savior's glorious body, if we have merited it by our clean and obedient lives, and thus shall we become like him.

Then is it not worth every effort in self-control to keep these bodies pure? Our ultimate destiny is to become like our Father in heaven and like our Elder Brother, Jesus our Savior. But we cannot reach it without purity, both of mind and body. So be honest with yourselves—be honest with the Lord who gives you this opportunity—and keep yourselves clean.

Now some among us may already have sinned. What about them? Is there any way back? Can they rise above their transgressions? Yes, they can. That is one of the most beautiful things about the gospel. The Lord gives us the opportunity of repentance.

"Have I any pleasure at all that the wicked should

die, saith the Lord God: and not that he should return from his ways, and live?

". . . if the wicked will turn from all his sins that he hath committed, and keep all my statutes, and do that which is lawful and right, he shall surely live, he shall not die.

"All his transgressions that he hath committed, they shall not be mentioned unto him: in his righteousness that he hath done shall he live." (Ezek. 18:23, 21-22.)

So the Lord holds out to us the gift of repentance and says:

"Come unto me, all ye that labour and are heavy laden, and I will give you rest. Take my yoke upon you, and learn of me; for I am meek and lowly in heart: and ye shall find rest unto your souls. For my yoke is easy, and my burden is light." (Matt. 11:28-30.)

It is infinitely light and easy when compared to the tremendous burden and slavery of sin. But as we take his yoke upon us, we must do so wholeheartedly and sincerely.

We cannot come halfway with him, for he severely condemns insincerity. We must come to him with all our heart, and with all our soul, and with all our strength, and with all our mind. We must not only turn from sin, but we must make reconciliation wherever that is necessary, and then for the rest of our lives keep his laws and statutes.

If we endure in righteousness to the end of our lives, our sins will not be mentioned to us again. In the righteousness that we have lived, shall we go on and receive his blessings. Then the Good Shepherd will say to us: "Well done, thou good and faithful servant; . . . enter thou into the joy of thy Lord." (Matt. 25:23.)

Chapter Eight

WHO CAN CHANGE THE LAW?

☐ Judy was greatly impressed by the lectures at the institute. She was certainly surprised to see Danny at each one of them. She still avoided him, but hoped deep in her heart that he was being converted to these standards of conduct.

Actually she had liked him a great deal, but by the time he was finished with his persuasions in the car that night, she had lost all respect for him.

But if he became converted to the Church and had his thinking about sex straightened out, he might yet have some promise.

The next lecture was scheduled for Friday night of the following week. Judy attended, and once again she saw Danny there. He waved to her, but she merely turned her head. She still wasn't ready for any resumption of their friendship.

The same speaker continued his series. This time he said:

There is a tendency in the world today to downgrade the law of chastity and say that there is a new code of morality now that permits the breakdown of standards and encourages one to "let yourself go."

Some educators, and even some clergymen, have adopted this view and promote it.

It is another evidence of the apostasy of the world from the teachings of Christ.

The Apostle Paul spoke of the apostasy from the gospel which began even in his day, but referred to it also on a much wider scale as it would affect the latter days. He said that this apostasy would be characterized by mankind becoming "lovers of their own selves, covetous, boasters, proud, blasphemers, disobedient to parents, unthankful, unholy,

"Without natural affection, trucebreakers, false accusers, incontinent, fierce, despisers of those that are good,

"Traitors, heady, highminded, lovers of pleasures more than lovers of God;

"Having a form of godliness, but denying the power thereof. . . ." (2 Tim. 3:2-5.)

Usually when people speak of an apostasy from the truth, they refer to changes in doctrines or a repudiation of certain beliefs. There has been an abundance of this.

Such changes have resulted in the organization of hundreds of churches with different creeds, rituals, and ordinances, many of them being highly contradictory.

But personal sin is as real an apostasy as any effort to change the law or break the everlasting covenant.

Consider Paul's words again: covetous, proud, blasphemers, false accusers, incontinent, without natural affection, lovers of pleasures more than lovers of God.

In other words, personal sin is as much an apostasy from Christ as an acceptance of false doctrines and man-made rituals.

But it is even worse when clergymen, pretending to represent the Christ, compound their apostasy by actually leading people into serious personal sin, at the same time asking them to practice creeds of their own invention that have no power to save.

Time magazine reported in its religious section that "the 20th Century's sexual revolution directly challenges Christianity's basic doctrines against immorality."

The magazine then goes on to say: "Some progressive church thinkers now advocate a 'new morality' to take account of these facts of life. What they propose is an ethic based on love rather than law, in which the ultimate criterion for right and wrong is not divine command but the individual's subjective perception of what is good for himself. . . ."

The article referred to 900 clergymen and students of religion recently gathered at Harvard University's Divinity School to ponder this so-called new morality. Many among those clergymen expressed the thought that this new moral concept which fosters licentious free love is what they call a "healthy advance" that now will relieve them of the responsibility of living the strict moral teachings of Christ.

An Episcopal minister, the Reverend Frederick C. Wood, speaking at Goucher College, Baltimore, told a group of young students that "sex is fun—premarital sex is beautiful—we all ought to relax and stop feeling guilty about our sexual activities, thoughts and desires." He was thus quoted by the Associated Press. These newspapers published his picture with the article on his attempt to reverse the divine law.

There are moves to ease up on laws regulating immoral behavior. Legislators are being asked to rule that adultery should no longer be considered a crime, that homosexuals and other deviates should be allowed to practice their depravities legally and without restriction, and that the age of consent for a child to enter public prostitution should be lowered to sixteen years.

This is one of the great evidences of the apostasy of mankind from the teachings of Christ.

To reject or try to change the moral law of God is to reject God. To leave the path of virtue as set forth by Christ is an apostasy from Christ. If any segment of Christianity attempts to change the moral law of God it will attack one of the most basic precepts of heaven and will thereby place itself in the role of anti-Christ.

Is God, who the scriptures say is the same yesterday, today, and forever (see Heb. 13:8), now changing his mind? Does Jesus no longer believe what he taught when he was on earth? He said that anyone who looks upon a woman with lust in his mind commits adultery in his heart. Note that he says that if we merely look upon another with lust, it is immoral.

Then what does he say about the completion of that act?

Does he call it beautiful as does this so-called Reverend Mr. Wood? Is the Savior now to retreat before the clerics who advocate free love?

Is he to admit that he was mistaken nineteen centuries ago and say that he was not as well informed as these modern clergymen? Will he now withdraw from his position and say that he was too strict for human nature and that he was not realistic?

Has Christ changed his mind?

Is he less understanding than the Reverend Mr. Wood in Baltimore?

Does he know less than Mr. Wood about the urges,

the drives, and the temptations of adolescent youth?

If Christ has not changed his mind, can the modern clerics change it for him?

Will he approve a reversal of his teachings?

Will he acknowledge the men who try to make the change? Will he recognize them as his ordained servants? Will he accept the churches that they represent? Will he call them his own?

Will he say that the primrose path is now the road to heaven or that it has become a modern version of the straight and narrow way?

Will he sanction the teaching of immorality to young boys and girls by men who claim to act in his holy name?

For any man to attempt to change the moral law is like trying to change the Deity himself.

It is to ask the Almighty to condone the petting, the necking, the wicked intimacies and perversions that go on in the back seats of automobiles, in motel and hotel rooms, and on park lawns and beaches.

It is asking him to sanction the illegal and murderous abortions that frequently follow.

It is inviting him to smile indulgently and sweetly on misguided young people as they sow the seeds of death and hell.

Easy morality is no morality at all. And certainly where there is no morality, there is no true Christianity either.

No one can make free love a doctrine and practice of the true Church of God, despite all that may be said by the 900 clergymen at Harvard Divinity School or by any other group of ministers or priests speaking before schools and youth groups.

Apostasy through immorality is at least as bad as returning to paganism.

God still says: "Thou shalt not commit adultery. . . ." (Exod. 20:14.)

Christ still says: ". . . whosoever looketh on a woman to lust after her hath committed adultery with her already in his heart." (Matt. 5:28.)

And Paul still says of those who deviate from the path of virtue into some of the great perversions, ". . . they which commit such things are worthy of death. . . ." (Rom. 1:32.)

In this modern day God has restored his pure gospel and his divine church. Again he teaches the truth about himself and the way to come back into his presence.

Part of that restoration is a restatement of the moral law.

Again comes his precept commanding: ". . . be ye clean, that bear the vessels of the Lord." (Isa. 52:11.)

Again he appeals for virtue—complete, chaste, unblemished purity—on the part of his followers, for no unclean thing can come into his presence.

By modern revelation he tells us that sex sin is next to murder in the divine category of crime. (See Alma 39:5.)

Virtue is as much a part of the restored gospel as are baptism and the resurrection.

Chastity is as vital to us as the law and the prophets.

The work of God cannot abide in the midst of iniquity. His people must not partake of the sins of Babylon or they will cease to be his people. Although we are in the world, we cannot indulge in its corruption.

We Latter-day Saints have a great modern message. We announce that God has appeared in our day. He has raised up modern prophets who speak for him, even as did Moses.

He has established his church again in this generation.

TWISTED STANDARDS

We are far gone on fancy euphemy. There are no lazy bums any more—only "deprived persons." It is impolite to speak of thugs. They are "underprivileged." Yet the swaggering, duck-tailed young men who boldly flaunt their gang symbols on their motorcycle jackets are far more blessed in creature comforts, opportunities for advancement, and freedom from drudgery than 90 percent of the children of the world. We have sown the dragon's teeth of pseudo-scientific sentimentality; and out of the ground has sprung the legion bearing switch-blade knives and bicycle chains.

Clearly, something is missing. Could it be the doctrine of individual responsibility?

—Jenkin Lloyd Jones
(From an address to the American Society of Newspaper Editors)

He is rearing a new and modern people, a priestly nation, a people of virtue and purity.

We have hundreds of thousands of youth in this heaven-blessed church, and they must be taught the restored truth. But they must know that this truth includes virtue as well as worship, and that there can be no true worship without chastity.

Youth of Zion:

Believe with all your heart in the restored gospel as given us through the Prophet Joseph Smith. Believe that this restored gospel is the way of truth and joy. Know that wickedness never was happiness, but obedience and chastity lead to the abundant life.

Know that virtue is a vital part of the restored gospel and can never be separated from it.

Know and understand that no man or set of men, whether clergymen, educators, or government officials, can change divine law. They are neither greater nor more intelligent than the Almighty.

The Lord asks you to be as clean as he is, so that you may be fit to enter into his presence and become like him, for that is your destiny.

Chapter Nine

WHAT OUR LEADERS SAY

☐ The next time Judy went to a class at the institute she remained afterward for a while, to talk further with Brother Reeves.

She told the institute director that she believed what she had been hearing about the law of chastity, and thanked him for arranging the lectures. She knew that many of her friends on the campus, even some of the Latter-day Saint students, needed such advice.

Judy told Brother Reeves that it was good to read what the scriptures had to say, but what about the present-day prophets? They are mouthpieces for God, are they not?

Brother Reeves assured her that they are, and he took down from a shelf some books with quotations from a few of the presidents.

All of them have discussed this subject vigorously, he told her, since it has always been a great challenge. However, not only are people to be chaste, they are to keep all of the other commandments of God as well.

The gospel is a way of life. It is the means by which we develop as the Lord intends. It provides the guidelines for us, showing us how we may become like our Father in heaven.

Therefore, as the mouthpieces of the Lord, the prophets of the Church have spoken out firmly regarding the law of chastity.

The Prophet Joseph Smith was not only one of our greatest advocates of this law, but it was through him that the Lord also spoke on this subject in our day, Brother Reeves continued.

He gave us section 42 of the Doctrine and Covenants, already referred to, but he also gave us a view of the ultimate destiny of unrepentant sex sinners. As he describes the hell of the eternal world and identifies those who shall go there, he says:

"These are they who are liars, and sorcerers, and adulterers, and whoremongers, and whosoever loves and makes a lie.

"These are they who suffer the wrath of God on earth.

"These are they who suffer the vengeance of eternal fire.

"These are they who are cast down to hell and suffer the wrath of Almighty God. . . ." (D&C 76:103-106.)

When he translated the Book of Mormon, the Prophet also provided the following from Alma as he spoke of the evil of sex sins:

"Know ye not, my son, that these things are an abomination in the sight of the Lord; yea, most abominable above all sins save it be the shedding of innocent blood or denying the Holy Ghost?" (Al. 39:5.)

And when he translated the words of Moroni, he referred to chastity and virtue as "that which was most dear and precious above all things." (Moro. 9:9.)

Brigham Young was outspoken on the subject. Said he: "Any man who humbles a daughter of Eve to rob her of her virtue, and cast her off dishonored and defiled, is her destroyer, and is responsible to God for his deed. If the refined Christian society . . . will tolerate such a crime, God will not; but he will call the perpetrater to an account. He will be damned; in hell he will lift up his eyes, being in torment, until he has paid the uttermost farthing, and made a full atonement for his sins." (*Discourses of Brigham Young*, p. 194.)

At another time he said:

"I would rather follow her to the grave, and send her home pure, than suffer my daughter to be prostituted. I will not suffer any female member of my family to be polluted through the corruptions of wicked men." (*Ibid.*)

"Ever since I knew that my mother was a woman I loved the sex and delighted in their chastity. The man who abuses, or tries to bring dishonor upon the female sex is a fool, and does not know that his mother and his sisters were women." (*Ibid.*)

President Joseph F. Smith, father of President Joseph Fielding Smith, said this:

"Sexual union is lawful in wedlock, and if participated in with right intent is honorable and sanctifying. But without the bonds of marriage, sexual indulgence is a debasing sin, abominable in the sight of Deity.

"Infidelity to marriage vows is a fruitful source of divorce, with its long train of attendant evils, not the least of which are the shame and dishonor inflicted upon unfortunate though innocent children. . . .

"It is a deplorable fact that society persists in holding women to stricter account than men in the matter of sexual offense. What shadow of excuse, not to speak of justification, can be found for this outrageous and cowardly discrimination? Can moral defilement be any the less filthy and pestilential in man than in woman? Is a male leper less to be shunned for fear of contagion than a woman similarly stricken?

"So far as woman sins, it is inevitable that she shall suffer, for retribution is sure, whether it be immediate or deferred. But in so far as man's injustice inflicts upon her the consequence of his offenses, he stands convicted of multiple guilt. And man is largely responsible for the sins against decency and virtue, the burden of which is too often fastened upon the weaker participant in the crime. . . ." (*Gospel Doctrine*, p. 309.)

"We believe in one standard of morality for men and women. If purity of life is neglected, all other dangers set in upon us like the rivers of waters when the flood gates are opened." (*Ibid.*, p. 313.)

To this Brother Reeves added:

"At no time has the Lord ever suggested that a sin in one person is less serious than in another. God is no respecter of persons. All are alike before him. He has but one standard of morals, and one law of chastity. To men and women alike that law says: 'Thou shalt not commit adultery.'

"The law is the same to all. The Lord does not make fish of one and fowl of another. He does not condemn one and condone another.

"He teaches that he delights in the chastity of women. But can he delight any less in the chastity of men who are his sons and to whom he has given his holy priesthood? Every holder of the priesthood is under the oath and covenant of the priesthood, which is an oath and covenant of righteousness, a solemn pledge to live by every word that proceedeth from the mouth of God. For some inexplicable reason man over the years has claimed a certain immunity in committing sin. But can any man justly claim that special privilege? And particularly can he with impunity drag his priesthood with him into the depths of sin in violation of his oath and covenant of righteousness?

"If sin can be greater in some than in others, then it is most serious in those who have the light and sin against it. It is most serious in those who are under covenant with God. And what Latter-day Saint, man or woman, is not under covenant, either in baptism or in the priesthood or both, not to mention the sacred ties of the sacrament of the Lord's supper?"

Brother Reeves read this from a sermon by President Heber J. Grant:

"I want to say at this time that the crying evil of the age is a lack of virtue. There is but one standard of morality in the Church of Christ. We have been taught, thousands of us who have been reared in this Church from our childhood days, that second only to murder is the sin of losing our virtue. I want to say to the fathers and to the mothers, and to the sons and daughters, in our Primary, in our Mutual Improvement Associations, in our seminaries and institutes, in Sunday School, in the Relief Society, and in all of our Priesthood quorums—I want it understood—that the use of liquor and tobacco is one of the chief means in the hands of the adversary whereby he is enabled to lead boys and girls from virtue.

"Nearly always those who lose their virtue, first partake of those things that excite their passions within them or lower their resistance and becloud their minds. Partaking of tobacco and liquor is calculated to make them a prey to those things which, if indulged in, are worse than death itself. There is no true Latter-day Saint who would not rather bury a son or a daughter than to have him or her lose his or her virtue—realizing that virtue is of more value than anything else in the wide world." (*Gospel Standards,* p. 55.)

President David O. McKay wrote:

"The test of true womanhood comes when woman stands at the court of chastity. All qualities are crowned by this most precious virtue of beautiful womanhood.

"It is the most vital part of the foundation of a happy married life. There is a general idea throughout the world that young men may sow their wild oats, but that young women should be chaperoned and guarded.

"But even in this matter of chaperonage there is too much laxity on the part of parents, if recent reports are to be relied on.

"In the Church of Jesus Christ there is but one standard of morality. No young man has any more right to sow his 'wild oats' in youth than has a young girl. He who comes to his bishop to ask for a recommend to take a pure girl to the altar is expected to give the same purity that he hopes to receive.

"A woman crowned with virtue is the highest, holiest, most precious gift to man, excepting only salvation offered in the gospel, and that forms a part of it. But a woman who barters her virtue is not one of the least of man's shames.

"Young men and women sometimes yield to indulgence for the sake of popularity. One who persistently bids for popularity at the expense of health and character is foolish.

"A man who stands behind a bar and swallows drink for the sake of popularity is paying a high price for a miserable product. Social popularity purchased in such a way and at such a price is not good enough for an honest man to wipe his feet upon.

"Indeed men who yield to temptation to seek popularity among friends lose the very thing they desire, while the boy who maintains his standards wins their respect."

Chapter Ten

THE
THREAT OF
DISEASE

☐ The next lecture at the institute brought out an even larger crowd. This time the subject was frightening; it dealt with the diseases that follow sexual impurities.

The lecturer said:

Much can and must be said about the spiritual aspects of morality and virtue. But we must understand also the negative side, including the dreadful effect unchastity has upon our physical health.

Since permissiveness has become so extensive, there has come with it the inevitable spread of disease. Promiscuity is filthy, and filth of every kind breeds disease. In the case of sex sin, it is venereal disease that comes in two major forms in America: syphilis and gonorrhea. Both are dreadful in the devastating effects they have upon human beings.

Each sexual contact with a promiscuous person is an open door to these diseases. Each promiscuous person can be a carrier. The diseases are transmitted directly by sex contact.

If trends continue in the future as they have done in the last few years, we will experience one of the worst epidemics we have ever known, worst in the type of illness, worst in the number of cases, in the number of deaths, and in the blindness, insanity, and crippling reactions that accompany it.

Promiscuity among teenagers is the main source of infection. It is not readily detected at first. Many infected teenagers say they had never been told of the connection between promiscuity and VD.

Doctors tell us that the disease is transmitted primarily through intimacy, but if an infected person has syphilis sores in his mouth, the disease also may be passed through kissing.

Syphilitic mothers can give the disease to unborn children, and even to infants after birth during the process of their normal care.

Seventy percent of the cases of this plague are not reported and are therefore not treated. Each reported case is known to involve an average of ten other persons. Less then eight percent of the cases of social disease are passed on by prostitutes. This points up the danger of youthful promiscuity in shocking terms.

Over 1,000 Americans die each *month* from venereal disease. Among those who are not treated, one in 200 becomes blind, one in 50 becomes insane, one in 25 is crippled, and one in 15 develops heart trouble.

The United States government spends about $70,000,000 annually to care for such unfortunates and an additional $30,000,000 for control.

Homosexuality is becoming one of the major means of spreading this disease.

There is no preventative—no drug known to man—that will protect human beings from this plague. One safeguard alone is effective: complete chastity.

The mounting statistics in this disease form an unassailable argument in favor of chastity. It is a disease of the unchaste. Young people particularly must be on the alert in its prevention. It can be contracted on a single date. One exposure to a carrier can spread it.

Statistics show that most cases come from indiscriminate association on dates among young people. It is the teenagers who have the highest incidence of this disease today.

The popular boy or the pretty girl with low morals may very easily be a carrier. Any loose person may be. The disease travels from one loose individual to another. It spreads as fast as smallpox, with a single exposure. But it is far more deadly and destructive. The disease is seldom contracted from using towels or public toilets, doctors say, for the virus dies quickly on exposure to the air. About the only way the disease may be passed on is by physical contact.

This makes promiscuity even more dangerous. And it makes tremendously risky dating persons with whom we are not well acquainted. Above all, it shows the utter idiocy of "giving in" to any boy or girl who may tempt us to do wrong.

The idea that social disease is easily wiped out, as has been boasted by those who attempt to justify their deviations, is not supported by medical men. A researcher associated with the Hollywood office of the Los Angeles City Health Department said on this point, as quoted in a Los Angeles newspaper:

"Many people have been lulled into believing that,

with the oncoming of the antibiotic wonder drugs, venereal disease would be eradicated. This was false optimism.

"The truth is," he continued, "that penicillin, chief weapon against VD, is losing its punch. Fifteen years ago 100,000 units of the drug were considered sufficient to effect a cure for gonorrhea. Today we are using doses of a million units and sometimes more. As our power to cure diminishes, VD is spreading. There has been a 200 percent increase of primary and secondary cases of syphilis in the nation in the past five years."

Then he said this frightening thing:

"Even more alarming is the fact that the greatest increase has been among young people. Half of those attending public VD clinics throughout the nation are kids, many of them only 15 and 16 years old. Last year there were more than 2,000 reported cases of VD among children under 14 years of age. There is no telling how many unreported cases."

A type of VD brought from Vietnam by promiscuous servicemen is completely resistant to penicillin, which is our best curative weapon.

Syphilis causes insanity, deafness, paralysis, blindness, heart disease, and death, the medical researchers explain. Gonorrhea causes sterility, blindness, and death, and more recently has been discovered to be a definite cause of certain types of arthritis.

The physical miseries of infected persons are appalling, but the mental anguish is even greater. The most staggering damage of all is to the spiritual qualities of persons who sin. The disease that afflicts the body is not the worst part of immorality. It is the damage to the soul, to one's standing in the eyes of God, and to future prospects of success in life through a blighted character.

Another researcher in this field said that the three

main causes of increased VD are: (1) a lowering of moral standards; (2) the shifting population; and (3) the rise in the number of homosexuals.

Then he said that the crying need is to educate our young people to maintain their high morals and their spiritual qualities as the only real protection against this menace.

LEGALIZING SIN

In some states efforts are being made to legalize certain forms of sin. Can that turn wickedness into righteousness?

Some would legalize drugs. Can that make the misuse of drugs good or honorable or uplifting? Can it take away the degradation that always accompanies it?

Does legalizing of gambling make it a righteous activity?

Does legalizing of homosexuality or other forms of immorality cleanse those perversions of their filth?

Human slavery was once legal. But was it good? Was it any less reprehensible under approval by law than it is now without such legal endorsement?

Then are immorality or misuse of drugs or consumption of liquor and tobacco made pure by legislative action?

God's laws remain firm. No man has the right to alter them.

The cry of the Lord to his people has always been: "Be ye clean that bear the vessels of the Lord."

Complete chastity is the only safeguard against this disease. No one may be vaccinated for it. No one can be sure of a cure once the disease has been contracted. No more are modern drugs as effective as once thought. The disease may break out again months and years after a person thinks he is cured. It may be passed on to helpless babies.

Our young people cannot be too careful about the persons with whom they associate. And they cannot be too careful about their habits as they date. No one knows when even one of the "elect" has fallen. Intimacies with those whom we think to be safe never should be allowed even on strictly physical grounds. If such a person tempts you to sin, he is already sinful himself. If he is sinful now, he most likely has fallen previously and may have contracted the disease then. He passes it on in his next offense. It is like an endless chain. No one can afford to be caught in such a net.

There is no substitute for complete chastity. It is the only safe path to follow. There is no fun in lowering the bars, only distress. Wickedness never was happiness. Joy comes only in purity.

When one visits the hospitals and sees the syphilitic blind, he knows that no amount of momentary thrill can compensate for loss of sight.

When he looks into the face and the eyes of those who have gone mad because this disease has eaten away their mental powers, he knows that no allurements can pay for a loss of sanity.

And when one looks at the syphilitic cripples, with gnarled fingers and toes and twisted limbs, he knows that the popularity offered in promiscuity can never settle the debt that nature levies against the unclean.

Cleanliness is next to Godliness, but it is also our only real protection against a plague that is now rising rapidly in the world as it kills and maims and blinds and sends people crazy.

Chapter Eleven

EXCUSING DEVIATIONS

☐ The institute lecturer next went on with this subject:

One of the most unfortunate things about young people in difficulty is that so many say they do not believe infractions of the moral laws are wrong.

So much has the so-called new morality been publicized that even some young Latter-day Saints have come to believe it.

Sex deviation is sinful! It is condemned by the Lord!

Virtue is not swayed by modern inventions, new philosophies, or expediencies of any kind.

It is a divine attribute and is eternal in its nature. It cannot be "watered down" by new devices coming under the guise of saving the world from overpopulation, population explosions, or whatever they may be named.

For years controversy has raged over means of preventing conception. Some phases of the dispute have been on religious grounds; others have pertained to medical research.

More recently science has developed the Pill, as an oral contraceptive is known.

The Pill does prevent conceptions in most cases, it is true, but there is now evidence of physical side effects, not published or heralded, but fought by doctors who now see the highly disturbing results of using this device.

When the press recently reported that cancer was a suspected side effect of one of the newly developed contraceptive pills, manufacture of that particular. drug was stopped. Dogs used in the experiment developed cancer. This particular drug professedly had not been used on human beings.

But what will be the side effects of the currently used and allegedly safe contraceptive pill?

Paralytic strokes and death by blood clots are now being reported in the thousands, directly related to the Pill.

The health hazards are not yet fully determined. Certain other efforts to interfere with the normal birth processes have ended in disaster. Women who have used fertility pills can testify to that.

When people take drugs to interfere with nature, they run the risk of physical dangers that are not yet fully determined. How many drugs are really safe? In small quantities, taken occasionally, some have left no injury. But used too freely, or combined with other substances, they may produce deadly results. Note, for example, what occurs in the combination of barbiturates and liquor. A drunken person may take sleeping pills, hoping to "sleep it off" and wake up in eternity. Many have done just that!

How do we know what will result from the present

wholesale and regular use of contraceptive pills? Those who take them should consider the possibilities.

Contraceptive pills also can prove to be the moral breakdown of the race. They have a side effect of moral corruption among young people from the early teens up to and including the married state.

Many girls who have been willing otherwise to indulge in illicit relations have been frightened to do so because of the dangers of pregnancy. They have given little thought to diseases or morals involved, but have just not wanted to have children out of wedlock.

A number of such individuals have hailed the Pill as the answer to their problem and have supposed that by using it they could live as loosely as they wished without running the greatly feared risk of pregnancy.

It is just as immoral to have illicit relations without pregnancy as it is when pregnancy follows. The act is adulterous whether children come or not.

No amount of medication can take the stain of immorality from illicit relationships, whether the use of such medication appears to be respectable or not.

The sex act under illicit circumstances is sin and is condemned by the Lord.

Without any reference to pills, devices, or innocent babes born from sinful acts, the scripture calls illicit sex relations violations of the law of God, next to murder in seriousness.

"This enlightened age" cannot change the laws of God, nor their intended meaning.

No matter how learned men become, they are not as wise as the Lord. It is true that some people in high places are immoral themselves and therefore condone promiscuity and encourage young people to walk in their footsteps.

It is likewise true that present-day philosophies having to do with a new morality are widely taught and encouraged. But they cannot change what the Lord has said.

People must keep themselves clean. Sex relations are for marriage, and only for marriage, and their purpose is for the rearing of good families. The use of contraceptives by unmarried people cannot take away the sinfulness of the illicit sex act.

Purity has been one of the great standards of the people of God from the beginning of time.

These principles hold equally true concerning homosexual acts. Such practices have been condemned by the Lord and his servants down through the ages. Both Old and New Testaments are vigorous in their condemnation of such sins.

Persons who participate in them can no more claim exemption from the moral law than the murderer can say he is not bound by the decree, "Thou shalt not kill."

Sin is sin, no matter in what guise it may appear.

The teaching that modern devices and inventions will now permit sex experience to become recreational, open to young and old alike without fear of consequences, is as satanic as anything the devil has ever perpetrated upon the human race.

As God provided procreation in the first place, he decreed that it should be pure and holy. Our bodies, as made by him, were to be temples of his Spirit, not playthings for lustful perversions.

We owe it to ourselves, to our families, and to the Almighty, to keep them so.

Chapter Twelve

MODESTY PROTECTS VIRTUE

☐ The Lord has spoken at various times pertaining to the virtues that he expects the Latter-day Saints to preserve. At one time he said, ". . . practise virtue and holiness before me." (D&C 38:24.) Still later he warned, ". . . ye must practise virtue and holiness before me continually." (D&C 46:33.) And while the Prophet was in Liberty Jail, the Lord spoke to him and said, ". . . let virtue garnish thy thoughts unceasingly; then shall thy confidence wax strong in the presence of God. . . ." (D&C 121:45.)

Inasmuch as he used the expression, "Practise virtue and holiness before me continually," the Lord not only spoke of virtue in the sense of chastity, but also in a broader sense, even as we speak of the different virtues represented in our Latter-day Saint standards.

The Lord seemed to include a general connotation

of the word *virtue* in his revelations. The dictionary gives as definitions courage, strength, valor, efficacy, excellence, merit, rectitude, purity, and chastity. The word *valor* is given as a synonym. Valor is defined as strength of mind that enables one to encounter danger firmly. It stands for gallantry, heroism, personal bravery, and courage.

What are the virtues the Lord had in mind when he urged the Saints to "let virtue garnish thy thoughts unceasingly" and "practise virtue and holiness before me continually"? We must practice the teachings of the Savior by upholding all of the standards of the Church. *Without the standards of the Church there is no holiness, nor any virtue either in its broader sense or in the strict definition of chastity.*

Let us note some of the standards of the Church that pertain to holiness and the various virtues the Lord expects to find in a Latter-day Saint. Let us mention just a few of them.

First, "We believe in being true." This is as essential as the gospel itself. Next, "We believe in being chaste." Benevolence, of course, is mentioned, and also patience, long-suffering, brotherly and sisterly kindness, forgiveness, charity, godliness, humility, and diligence.

Are our virtues, our standards, in danger? Is there need for valor and courage and strength in meeting such dangers today?

Do you know what tempts boys to molest girls today more than any other one thing? It is the mode of dress of girls who often wear extremely abbreviated clothes even on the streets, who wear dresses well above the knees, whose clothing about the bust is often so tight and revealing that it nearly takes the breath away from the boys who look at it.

It is the low-cut evening dress, which permits a boy to

dance all evening gazing down into a half-concealed but half-disclosed bosom, thus setting him on fire with an unholy desire.

It is often the very skimpy gymnasium suits girls are forced to wear in their physical education classes at school.

When the boys are coming into their teens and reaching maturity, and such sights are placed before their eyes, almost like an invitation, can we blame them—any more than we would the girls who tempt them—if they take advantage of those girls?

Unfortunately, many of these young women are innocent victims of a bad situation. From infancy they wear but little clothing. As they reach early childhood there is still little clothing, and so on into young adulthood. They are taught that this is the style, and they must follow it. They become accustomed to exposing themselves. It is all they seem to know, and who is to blame? Who permits them to dress in this manner? Who buys their clothes? Who is it that permits them to wear lipsticks and high heels even before they reach their teens? Who permits them to go dating at twelve, thirteen, fourteen, and fifteen with little restriction or supervision?

And who permits not only this early dating but steady dating as well, steady dating which so often leads to early intimacies, degradation, and loss of this precious virtue of which we speak and which frequently results in early marriages which almost always break up, even while the youngsters are still in their teens?

The Lord says we are to garnish our thoughts with virtue unceasingly. Can a boy's thoughts be garnished with virtue as he gazes at her limbs so fully exposed by these short, short skirts of today?

Are the girls' thoughts garnished with virtue when they wear revealing clothing? Are their thoughts garnished with virtue while they engage in petting, and then hope for an early marriage to cover up their indiscretions?

A recent national publication carried an editorial discussing this subject, and among other things it said that we must face the fact that more and more American women are unwittingly inviting sex crimes. It was estimated that at least half of the reported rape cases could have been avoided had the victim shown more discretion and good judgment. The peculiarly American system of encouraging our girls to be attractive and alluring, or training them to be seductive, and then telling them of course that they must draw an uncrossable line, was considered as a destructive system.

The editorial said that the entire concept of training our young women to "both lure and repel, simultaneously," is responsible for irreconcilable conflicts. A girl is encouraged to believe that the number of her dates and the amount of passion she arouses in them may in many cases be the total measure of her success as a female.

And then the editorial calls for a new American heroine, not one who is a sweater girl, whose main claim to fame seems to be the shape of her body and how much of it she is willing to reveal, but a national heroine of virtue and cleanliness, one who is willing to put her sex appeal in the background and put forward her wit, her charm, her intelligence, and her integrity.

If the women and girls of the Church would practice the kind of virtue the Lord speaks of, they could change this situation. If they had the valor and the courage, they would live up to the Church standards of decency and right.

The styles of today are immodest, but many women follow them and reject the counsel of Church leaders. So whom do they sustain, whom do they place first in their lives? When it comes to styles, it certainly is not the leaders of the Church, and yet modesty is the first line of defense for chastity.

When our girls and boys lose their virtue, we cry to high heaven and wonder why this should ever come to our families, forgetting that in our desire to be fashionable we have set aside modesty, which is the great protector of virtue.

As long as we turn away from modesty in dress and follow the way of the world in style, just that long will we pay the price in a breakdown of morals among the younger generation.

Have we the courage to correct this condition? We can have a style of our own, a modest one! We are over three million people and no longer a small minority.

But in this we would not be alone. Millions of other women are as modest as we would like our women to be. Recently, one of the colleges of the United States, a non-Latter-day Saint school, had a style show in which every dress shown was as modest as if it had been cut out by the General Authorities themselves. There are many sensible and decent people in the world who would support us.

Why can we not join with them rather than with those who are so evil-minded that they design styles to emphasize sex, knowing very well that such an appeal is an invitation to sin?

Chapter Thirteen

THE VALUE OF STANDARDS

☐ An acceptance of the standards of the Church is vital to our progress in the kingdom of God. They determine our actions, they dictate our mode of life, and they determine how we will live under the various circumstances that face us.

Standards are based upon virtue, taking that word in its broadest sense. Without virtue, we become enemies to God.

Without virtue there is no purity.

Without purity there is no strength.

Without strength there is no character.

Without character there is no true spirituality.

Without spirituality there is no salvation in the kingdom of God.

In short, faith without the works of virtue is dead.

And naturally there are neither the works of virtue nor virtue itself if there are no standards.

Latter-day Saint standards not only include virtue in its principal meaning, but they also include the so-called little things that lead up to their violation.

These little things often in turn lead to smoking and drinking and the use of harmful drugs, which subsequently and frequently result in a loss of chastity.

For example, have you ever seriously thought about what a cigarette means to a Latter-day Saint? It means more to us than it does to other people. Some of you will say that you do not see why, that you have friends in other churches who smoke, and they seem to get along all right, and their churches do not criticize them for it, and you do not see why our church takes the attitude it does on this subject.

Just remember, if you will, that the Lord has not spoken to your young friends in the other churches, nor to the heads of their churches, giving them any divine revelation directing them to abstain from these harmful things. In their churches they do not even accept the principle of modern revelation.

But with us, it is entirely different. God has spoken to us by his latter-day prophets. He has given us modern-day revelation, declaring that tobacco is not good for man. That is the word and the will of the Lord to the Latter-day Saints. Whenever we turn our backs upon that principle, to that extent we turn our backs upon the Lord.

The average young American is an individual who loves freedom, wants to be his own boss, and does not like to have other people regulate his life for him. But some young people misunderstand their independence, and in a spirit of misunderstanding say, "Well, if I want to smoke, that is my business. I have a perfect right to. It is a free country, isn't it?" But in submitting to the enslaving influence of nicotine, they contribute to a loss of the very freedom they talk about.

If you adopt the cigarette habit, it will, in large measure, determine the kind of life you are going to live, the kind of friends you will have, the kind of person you are going to marry, even the kind of children you may have. Do you regard that as an extreme statement? Let us think about it for a few moments.

If, at your house, you happen to take a newspaper or a magazine that carries cigarette advertising, and those alluring advertisements tempt you to smoke and try to make you think that it is smart to puff on a cigarette, and if you fall for that temptation, what is the first thing you do?

You brush to one side all the teachings of your parents, your church, and your friends who love you. Instead, you take the advice of a tobacco merchant who has no more interest in you than to get what money he can out of you by making you a slave to his product.

And then, you tell yourself, "I think I will buy some cigarettes." And so, with a guilty conscience, and feeling as if the eyes of the whole world are upon you, you go and buy your first package of cigarettes.

Then you wonder where you are going to smoke them. You do not want to smoke them in front of your parents because you know it is wrong, and you know it would break their hearts. You do not want to smoke in front of your nonsmoking friends because you know what they would tell you.

And so, you go someplace where neither your friends nor your parents can see you. Then you open the package, and you take out that first cigarette, put it in your mouth, and light it. Then you make a great discovery: You find that by sucking on one end of that cigarette, with the light on the other, you can actually get smoke out of it; and having read what you have in the advertisements, and having puffed away on that cigarette, the whole operation inflates your ego.

So you throw back your head, and you blow the smoke in the air, and you say, "Well, I really must be somebody."

You want to smoke some more, inasmuch as you have fallen for that temptation, but you do not want to do it in private all the time, and you do not want to be the only smoker in a nonsmoking crowd, so you seek out other people who smoke, so you can smoke with them. It may be that you already have some smoking friends and that they were the ones who provided those first cigarettes and that you began to smoke with them. In either case, you begin breaking off your connections with your nonsmoking friends and start to form your associations among smokers. And in this way, your cigarettes begin to choose your friends for you. And it is the same way with drugs. You seek out other drug users as your companions.

One of the very difficult things about this is that the habits of smokers so often do not stop with smoking, but they include drinking and unwise partying as well. And when you start going with people who do those things, it will not be very long before you are doing the same things they are, and in that way the cigarette lays the foundation on which you form other evil habits.

If you are going to be a smoker, you realize that you are breaking one of the commandments of God, and you do not feel good about it. You know that over in the ward they speak about the Word of Wisdom every once in a while, and now that you are a smoker you do not like to hear about the Word of Wisdom. You have heard about it all your life, and you do not want your conscience to hurt you any more than it already does, so you tell yourself you had better stay away from your meetings. You begin to realize that for a Latter-day Saint, worship and smoking just do not go together. And so the cigarette persuades you to stay away from church.

When you were small, your parents taught you to pray, and you prayed with more or less regularity all your life. But now that you are a smoker, you feel out of harmony with the Lord and you hesitate to go to him in prayer.

You begin to discover that, for a Latter-day Saint, cigarettes undermine faith and interfere with prayer. And as a child who has been hurt avoids the instruments that hurt him, so you with a smarting conscience shy away from your religious duties. You have come to know that spirituality and smoking are incompatible. And so the cigarette persuades you to stop praying.

Your parents also taught you to pay tithing on everything you earned, but now that you do not go to church very often and you are not very proud of your church connections, you stop paying your tithing. "What is the use?" you ask yourself. You say, "This tithing money itself would buy quite a few cigarettes; they cost real money these days." Rather an expensive habit you have picked up! And so the cigarette persuades you to stop paying your tithing.

When you get old enough to get married, you ask yourself, "Whom shall I marry?" If you are a boy you say, "Will it be Helen or Jane or Elizabeth?" And if you are a girl, you ask yourself, "Will it be Tom or Dick or Harry?" And then you tell yourself that you like Tom better than Harry, and Jane better than Elizabeth. And why do you like them better? Because they are in the crowd you go with; you know, the smoking crowd. And they do the things that you do.

They are like you. Why, you would not even think of marrying one of your former friends in the nonsmoking crowd. How ridiculous! Why, he would not smoke with you—would not even take a cocktail, and he would not neck, and he would not pet, and he would not party around. Why, you would not marry one of them!

You are going to marry one of your own crowd, one of the smoking crowd. And then, if you want to sit down together and smoke together you can, and there is no embarrassment—so you tell yourself. There is nobody to get after you if you fill the house full of tobacco smoke, and no one to nag at you if your cigarette burns a hole in the couch, or if you drop hot ashes on the new rug. So your cigarette has helped to choose the person you marry.

What kind of home will you have? There will not be much faith in it, because the cigarettes have already undermined your faith. And you will not say very many prayers, because the cigarettes have taken care of that, too. And there will not be much church activity in your house, because the cigarettes have checked that off also. So you will have a worldly home with precious little spirituality in it. Is that really the kind of home you want?

Will you have any children in that home? If you are like many of the smoking young people of today, you will not have any children. One of them recently said, "Why, a squawking kid would cramp my style! Do you think I am going to stay up and walk the floor in the middle of the night with a squealing baby in my arms? None of that for me!"

And so the cigarette may help to rob you of one of the greatest blessings that God gives us in this life: the privilege of having little children.

But suppose by some chance you do have children— what will they be like? Why, they will be just like you. They will not believe very much in God, because you will not make religion very important in their lives. They will not say very many prayers, because you will not teach them how. And they will not go to Church much, because you do not. And when they get a little older, they will acquire the other habits that you have, and they will be just about like you. So the cigarette determines in large measure the kind of children you will have.

Do you not see, young people of the Church, how the cigarette can mark out your life for you—point the path for you to follow? Are you willing to surrender to the tyranny of a cigarette? Are you willing to allow a cigarette to determine in such large measure the kind of life you are going to live? Are you going to allow a cigarette to choose the kind of friends you have, the kind of person you will marry—even the kind of children you may have? Are you, as a young Latter-day Saint, willing to allow a cigarette to determine your attitude toward God?

Let us ask one other thing: What do you think of religion, anyway? Is it worthwhile? Is it worth the trouble we go to? Does it do any good in the world? Or would we be better off without it?

There once was an advertisement that asked this question: "How would you like to live in a town in which there were no churches?" And then it listed the crime and the violence and the debauchery and the filth and the heartbreak and the sorrow and the disappointment associated with persons who reject the soul-elevating, character-building influence of true religion.

Would you like to live in a town in which there were no churches? Bring it right down to your own case and ask yourself about it. Would you like to live a life in which there was no religion? Do you really want the degrading influence of the irreligious? That influence is just as deadly for an individual as it is for a whole town.

Choose for yourself: Do you want to live a life without God? The cigarette would like you to. So would drugs and liquor. But remember, you can never live successfully without the Lord. Many have tried, and all have failed.

And so we come back to the question: Have you ever really considered what a cigarette means to a Latter-day Saint?

You who smoke now, do not make the mistake of supposing that the Church is against you, because it is not. It only desires your welfare, and it hopes and prays for the day when you will declare your independence from the slavery of nicotine.

And you who do not smoke, before you take that first cigarette ask yourself, "Will it help me or hurt me?" Think it over carefully, and may God guide you in your thinking.

Chapter Fourteen

PURE PARENTHOOD

Pure parenthood is next to Godhood.

Who can look at a good mother without knowing that her part in reproducing life is sacred?

And who can observe a good father as he relates to his family without also knowing that his is a divinely appointed responsibility?

On Mother's Day each year we extol the virtues of her who gave us birth. And on Father's Day we honor the man who has given us so much in this world. And why? Because good parenthood is closely related to the divine.

It is with this thought in mind that we must resolve to preserve and protect our own procreative powers, because procreation means parenthood. Children come of it—these little innocent babes who find themselves completely at the mercy of their elders, but who have come so recently from the presence of God in heaven.

As we measure our appreciation and love for our own parents, is there anything for which we are more grateful than to know that we are wellborn, that we have honorable names and clean blood in our veins?

Are we not deeply thankful that our parents so lived the law of virtue that no stain left its blemish upon us as we came into the world?

Do we not owe that same blessing to our offspring?

Would we not hope that our children will revere us as we revere our parents? And could that come without honorable legitimate birth?

In speaking of parenthood, President David O. McKay wrote the following about mothers:

"Motherhood is the one thing in all the world which most truly exemplifies the God-given virtues of creating and sacrificing. Though it carries the woman close to the brink of death, motherhood also leads her into the very realm of the fountains of life and makes her co-partner with the Creator in bestowing upon eternal spirits mortal life.

"Artists may make new visions real; poets express thoughts never known before or dress old ones in a more becoming garb; engineers may transform deserts into bounteous fields and fill them with prosperous towns and thriving villages; scientists may discover new elements and by various combinations thereof create means contributive either to progress or destruction—all these are in a measure revealers of unknown things; but the mother who, in compliance with eternal law, brings into the world an immortal spirit occupies first rank in the realm of creation.

"Motherhood is just another name for sacrifice. From the moment the wee, helpless babe is laid on the pillow beside her, Mother daily, hourly, gives of her life to her loved one. It has been aptly said that babes draw strength at first from her bosom but always from her heart.

"All through the years of babyhood, childhood, and youth, aye, even after her girls themselves become mothers and her sons, fathers, she tenderly, lovingly sacrifices for them her time, her comfort, her pleasures, her needed rest and recreation, and, if necessary, health and life itself! No language can' express the power and beauty and heroism of a mother's love.

"For all this consecrated devotion, she asks nothing in return. If her love is reciprocated, she is content; but if not, and her wayward child with poisoned feelings turns heedlessly from her, she still loves on, giving yearning and solicitude far more than the recreant deserves.

"No, she asks nothing in return; nothing for the roses she has transplanted from her own cheeks to those of her darling; nothing for the hours of vigilance during days and nights of sickness; nothing for the thousand self-denials and sacrifices that had to be made that the children in their 'teens' might receive proper schooling and 'appear well' with their comrades; nothing for the heartaches caused by thoughtless word or act of wayward youth.

"No, for all this and a thousand other things incident to motherhood, Mother asks nothing; but she deserves much. For kindness she deserves kindness; for tenderness, she should be given tenderness; for self-sacrifice, a little self-denial on the part of the children; for love, she should in return have love.

"In the most agonizing moment of his life, Christ thought of his mother. In this as in all other things, the Savior of men has given us an example. As Mother gave us our life 'at the peril of her own,' so we should be pleased, no matter what our desires, our condition, or our pains to give such of our time, our thought, our words, our means, as may be necessary to Mother's contentment and peace.

"To each mother's son or daughter, we would say: you need no suggestions on how to make your mother happy on Mother's Day as on every day in the year. If you order a white carnation to be given her, she will be pleased; if you tell her in a letter of your appreciation and love, she will shed tears of happiness; but if you keep the spotless character and purity of soul she has given you, she will rejoice as the most blessed of mothers." (*Gospel Ideals,* pp. 456-57.)

There is something saintly about good mothers, for they are in very deed the partners of God. To preserve that sanctity is one of the greatest obligations of the human race.

The great minds of the world have always honored womanhood and have placed a halo of respect about true motherhood. Who can forget what Lincoln said about his mother, or the attitude of Washington toward his parents? Who can forget Benjamin Franklin, the Adamses, Hancock, and LaFayette, and the great honor in which they held the opposite sex? They placed woman on a pedestal of almost worshipful esteem.

Good mothers are angelic. They deserve all the honor we can bestow upon them. They not only "rock the cradle," but are a redeeming influence in an otherwise difficult world. But if motherhood descends from its pedestal, a dark shadow is cast over all concerned.

What promiscuous man really respects womanhood? Who of them can honor any mother while lacking a decent regard for the proper status of womanhood?

And who can respect a father who is not virtuous and who shows little or no respect for his own family?

There can be no true honor for parents without an equal regard for chastity. Good parents are the personification of chastity. They are virtuous, self-sacrificing, and truly God-fearing.

There is but one way to preserve true parenthood in this wicked world, and that is to re-enshrine virtue in its proper place.

Without chastity, angelic motherhood as Lincoln knew it can never be achieved nor can mothers ever come to really know the love of God or a true affection for their own offspring.

And without righteousness, can any man ever hope to be regarded as a true servant of God? Can any man fulfill his priesthood destiny without being a clean and honorable parent?

To preserve our sense of values, to honor our mothers and fathers, and to protect the perpetuity of the race, let us unitedly strive to establish universal respect for virtue itself, the kind of virtue represented by all good parents.

Who of us would wish to be a child of promiscuity?

Chapter Fifteen

THE PLACE OF MARRIAGE

☐ When God provided marriage for Adam and Eve in the Garden of Eden, he gave us a pattern for our own lives.

Their marriage was an eternal one. It was performed before death came into the world. It continued after their resurrection.

Our marriage may be just as eternal as theirs. It is the plan of God that it should be. And our destiny is no different from that of our first parents. It is to become like God.

But the Lord has his own way of bringing it about.

It is accomplished through temple marriage, which is one of the saving ordinances of the gospel. Without it we cannot be exalted in the heavens above. It is as much a saving ordinance as baptism. It is as essential to our eternal advancement as the resurrection.

Therefore, as Latter-day Saints, we should be satisfied with nothing less.

When we remember that the Lord's plan is to project family life into eternities, and that family life is based completely upon marriage, then we must realize that our marriage must be of an eternal nature. It must be projected through death and the resurrection in order to survive and function in the eternities.

That brings us then to God's mode of matrimony, which means a wedding in the temple. Civil marriage will not satisfy us, for it ends with death. Since civil marriages are for mortal life only, death actually and literally becomes a divorce action and annuls them.

The Lord explained this in section 132 of the Doctrine and Covenants. Said he:

"Therefore, if a man marry him a wife in the world, and he marry her not by me nor by my word, and he covenant with her so long as he is in the world and she with him, their covenant and marriage are not of force when they are dead, and when they are out of the world; therefore, they are not bound by any law when they are out of the world.

"Therefore, when they are out of the world they neither marry nor are given in marriage; but are appointed angels in heaven, which angels are ministering servants, to minister for those who are worthy of a far more, and an exceeding, and an eternal weight of glory." (Verses 15-16.)

When we read section 131 of the Doctrine and Covenants we learn that the celestial kingdom is subdivided into three sections. The Lord speaks of the highest and the lowest but gives us no revelation with respect to the other portion.

He does, however, make it clear that without temple marriage we cannot enter the highest glory, which is exaltation. Without it, he says, we come to the end of our kingdom; we cannot have an increase.

This seems like hard doctrine, but it is amply supported in the verses quoted above.

A person who rejects temple marriage may become a "ministering servant" to those who are worthy of a higher glory, or exaltation, "but that is the end of his kingdom, he cannot have an increase."

Then the Lord gives the reason:

"For these angels did not abide my law; therefore, they cannot be enlarged, but remain separately and singly [unmarried], without exaltation, in their saved condition, to all eternity. . . ." (Verse 17.)

This is frightening doctrine, but it points up the fact, as the Lord did to Nicodemus, that the gospel ordinances are as essential as living the good life; both are required to achieve the fulness of the Lord's blessings.

On this point it is well to read a verse or two in section 76 of the Doctrine and Covenants, which relates to our status in the world to come.

As is well-known, this section teaches the doctrine of the three degrees of glory and points out who among us will go to each of these glories.

When the Lord refers to the terrestrial kingdom, he speaks of some—presumably Latter-day Saints—who have the testimony of Jesus but are not valiant in their attitude toward it. These, he says, will not be given celestial glory but will be assigned to a lower place. So the scripture says:

"Wherefore, they are bodies terrestrial, and not bodies celestial, and differ in glory as the moon differs from the sun.

"These are they who are not valiant in the testimony of Jesus; wherefore, they obtain not the crown over the kingdom of our God." (Verses 78-79.)

Scriptures like these should make us all alert to our situation. If we are in the Church and are not valiant in our testimony, meaning that we are not living the commandments or being active in the Church, we lose our crowns if we do not repent, and we will be assigned to the terrestrial glory.

If we reject temple marriage, we will be excluded from exaltation. To become perfect like God requires constant devotion. We cannot achieve perfection by imperfect means.

As Jesus said, we are either for him or against him, and if we are not for him, we are classed with his opponents. (Matt. 12:30.)

So if we believe in our glorious religion, if we desire to reach our destiny, we must not deviate from the gospel plan. Like Paul we must fight a good fight, we must keep the faith, and we must finish our course just as the Lord provides that we should. (2 Tim. 4:7.)

A discussion of temple marriage should also include mention of worthiness to enter the temple.

All who ask for recommends to enter the temple are interviewed by both their bishops and stake presidents and must meet all conditions of worthiness or they cannot enter that sacred place. And of course if they do not enter the temple, they are not given its blessings.

Again the importance of the worthy life is pointed up. And again the need for repentance, if we have sinned, comes to the fore.

The Lord offers salvation to all—if we will but serve him. And in each case, it is a personal decision. But we must earn our blessings.

What is of most worth to us, the blessings the Lord has to offer or the allurements of the world?

Which of us, knowing the facts, would exchange our eternal opportunities for the very questionable "enjoyment" of a few wicked moments?

Which of us would knowingly allow depravity to shut the temple doors against us?

And what of our children? Should they not have the blessings of the temple? Being wellborn should certainly include an eternal sealing to their own parents, with the blessings of knowing that they will belong to their own family forever.

So it becomes more and more evident that living a good life makes sense from every standpoint.

One other thing should be mentioned here. Always when we speak of the essential nature of temple marriage, the question arises: what of the faithful young women who never have an opportunity for a good marriage? Can they be exalted?

Of course the immediate answer is that all faithful persons will receive exaltation, whether they are married in this life or not.

These faithful girls need not worry on this point. They must know and realize that the Lord will provide for them if they will continue to keep the commandments for the rest of their lives.

Every good girl will be cared for by the Lord. Who knows but what her young man was killed in the war, or was struck as a child by a car, or died of some childhood disease?

A bad marriage is worse than no marriage at all for a faithful girl. Everyone should seek for a good marriage— a temple marriage—to a faithful partner with whom to walk through time and eternity.

If the faithful are not married in this life—and many

are not—the Lord will provide for them in eternity that they may enjoy the highest blessings. All of this—*if* they remain faithful to the gospel standards.

Chapter Sixteen

HAVE WE THE COURAGE?

☐ One thing now became uppermost in Judy's mind. It was the question: Have I the courage to live as I should?

The young men and women on the campus were generally quite free and easy with each other. Among them there were few restrictions of the type she was now considering.

What if they dropped her from their social activities?

What if she were left a "wallflower"?

What would she do if she had no more dates?

She had turned Danny away, and it was a good thing: good for him, in that he now is studying the gospel, and good for her for it prevented a serious mistake.

Would she want Danny back? The more she thought of him, the more she decided against him. She wished him the best and hoped that he would join the Church, but she would always distrust him, she told herself, because of her experience in the car.

Of course there was repentance. But since he had attempted to take liberties with her, had he also taken liberties with other girls? And how far had he gone with them? Had he lost his virtue? Would she want to marry a man who had sinned with another woman, even though he was repentant? Did she not owe to her own children an unblemished parenthood on both sides, her own and her husband's?

She was sure now that if she lived righteously, the Lord would take care of her. She decided that a bad marriage was worse than no marriage at all, and she would have faith that the Lord would provide for her a mate who would be as clean as she was.

But it would take courage. She knew that. And yet she now was sufficiently determined to live the Lord's way that the fun on the campus, the kids in her classes, somehow didn't matter much any more.

Then she recalled the institute. There were nearly two hundred Latter-day Saints on the campus, and most of them were enrolled there.

She herself had not attended classes at the institute very regularly, but since becoming better acquainted with Dr. Reeves, she was sure she would do better in that regard.

And there she could meet more of the LDS young people who would have her standards and would welcome her to their group. It is wonderful to be with your own kind.

She made the decision. Her social life would be in the institute program and with the young people enrolled there.

Living her religion would be easier if she stayed more with others who believed as she did. They would not present the temptations that the other students did. Rather, they would encourage her in the better way.

The institute social programs were as clean as the classes, and they would be fun. It would be fun just to be with clean people and do the things they do.

Seeing things in this new light, she felt it would not be any loss to her to give up dating with nonmembers. She knew now what she wanted in life, and it was to be found only in the Church.

Would it take courage, then? Yes, but it was the right decision that she needed most. And she made it.

CHOOSE THE RIGHT!

Choose the right! let no spirit of digression
Overcome you in the evil hour;
There's the right and the wrong to every question,
Be safe through inspiration's power.

Choose the right! there is peace in righteous
    doing;
Choose the right! there's safety for the soul;
Choose the right in all labors you're pursuing;
Let God and heaven be your goal.

INDEX